Ministry to the Sick

According to the use of
The Episcopal Church
as set forth in
The Book of Common Prayer

 CHURCH

Compiled and Edited by Leo Malania
Church Publishing Incorporated, New York

Certificate

I certify that The Ministration to the Sick, and the other rites and prayers from The Book of Common Prayer included in this edition, have been compared with the texts approved by the General Convention of 1976 and that they conform thereto.

Charles Mortimer Guilbert
Custodian of the Standard Book of Common Prayer
June, 1978

Contents

Note

This edition has been compiled for the purpose of providing a convenient collection of materials for the use of a hospital chaplain, or of a lay person, deacon, or priest visiting patients only occasionally, whether in hospitals or in homes. All the rites and prayers have been drawn from The Book of Common Prayer. Biblical readings are

reprinted from The Revised Standard Version of the Bible, by permission of the copyright holders, the Division of Christian Education of the National Council of the Churches of Christ in the United States of America, to whom grateful acknowledgment is here recorded.

An effort has been made to ensure that this edition is sufficiently comprehensive to meet a variety of needs: from a bedside celebration, to one for ambulatory patients, with nurses, doctors, and visitors present; from forms for a conditional or emergency baptism, to a service at the time of death, or a thanksgiving for recovery or the birth of a child.

An effort was also made to give some taste to the rich variety of The Book of Common Prayer by including traditional and contemporary rites for the Celebration of the Holy Communion.

It is assumed that when services are held in a hospital chapel, a sufficient number of Prayer Books will be available; but even in chapels many patients might prefer to hold a less bulky volume.

Ministration to the Sick

In case of illness, the Minister of the Congregation is to be notified.

At the Ministration, one or more parts of the following service are used, as appropriate; but when two or more are used together, they are used in the order indicated. The Lord's Prayer is always included.

Part One of this service may always be led by a deacon or lay person.

When the Laying on of Hands or Anointing takes place at a public celebration of the Eucharist, it is desirable that it precede the distribution of Holy Communion, and it is recommended that it take place immediately before the exchange of the Peace.

The Celebrant begins the service with the following or some other greeting

Peace be to this house (place), and to all who dwell in it.

Part I. Ministry of the Word

One or more of the following or other passages of Scripture are read

General *(page 93)*

2 Corinthians 1:3–5 (God comforts us in affliction)
Psalm 91 (He will give his angels charge over you)
Luke 17:11–19 (Your faith has made you well)

Penitence *(page 96)*

Hebrews 12:1–2 (Looking to Jesus, the perfecter of our faith)
Psalm 103 (He forgives all your sins)
Matthew 9:2–8 (Your sins are forgiven)

When Anointing is to follow *(page 99)*

James 5:14–16 (Is any among you sick?)
Psalm 23 (You have anointed my head with oil)
Mark 6:7, 12–13 (They anointed with oil many that were sick)

When Communion is to follow *(page 102)*

1 John 5:13–15 (That you may know that you have eternal life)
Psalm 145:14–22 (The eyes of all wait upon you, O Lord)
John 6:47–51 (I am the bread of life)

After any Reading, the Celebrant may comment on it briefly.

Prayers may be offered according to the occasion.

The Priest may suggest the making of a special confession, if the sick person's conscience is troubled, and use the form for the Reconciliation of a Penitent. (See pp. 27 and 29)

Or else the following general confession may be said. (Other forms of the general confession may be found on pages 36 and 38)

Most merciful God,
we confess that we have sinned against you
in thought, word, and deed,
by what we have done,
and by what we have left undone.
We have not loved you with our whole heart;
we have not loved our neighbors as ourselves.
We are truly sorry and we humbly repent.
For the sake of your Son Jesus Christ,
have mercy on us and forgive us;
that we may delight in your will,
and walk in your ways,
to the glory of your Name. Amen.

The priest alone says

Almighty God have mercy on you, forgive you all
your sins through our Lord Jesus Christ, strengthen
you in all goodness, and by the power of the Holy
Spirit keep you in eternal life. *Amen.*

A deacon or lay person using the preceding form substitutes "us" for "you" and "our" for "your."

Part II. Laying on of Hands and Anointing

*If oil for the Anointing of the Sick is to be blessed, the
Priest says*

O Lord, holy Father, giver of health and salvation:
Send your Holy Spirit to sanctify this oil; as your
holy apostles anointed many that were sick and
healed them, so may those who in faith and repentance receive this holy unction be made whole;
through Jesus Christ our Lord, who lives and reigns
with you and the Holy Spirit, one God, for ever and
ever. *Amen.*

The following anthem is said

Savior of the world, by your cross and precious blood you have redeemed us;
Save us, and help us, we humbly beseech you, O Lord.

The Priest then lays hands upon the sick person, and says one of the following

N., I lay my hands upon you in the Name of the Father, and of the Son, and of the Holy Spirit, beseeching our Lord Jesus Christ to sustain you with his presence, to drive away all sickness of body and spirit, and to give you that victory of life and peace which will enable you to serve him both now and evermore. *Amen.*

or this

N., I lay my hands upon you in the Name of our Lord and Savior Jesus Christ, beseeching him to uphold you and fill you with his grace, that you may know the healing power of his love. *Amen.*

If the person is to be anointed, the Priest dips his thumb in the holy oil, and makes the sign of the cross on the sick person's forehead, saying

N., I anoint you with oil in the Name of the Father, and of the Son, and of the Holy Spirit. *Amen.*

The Priest may add

As you are outwardly anointed with this oil, so may our heavenly Father grant you the inward anointing of the Holy Spirit. Of his great mercy, may he forgive you your sins, release you from suffering, and restore you to wholeness and strength. May he deliver you from all evil, preserve you in all goodness, and bring you to everlasting life; through Jesus Christ our Lord. *Amen.*

In cases of necessity, a deacon or lay person may perform the anointing, using oil blessed by a bishop or priest.

If communion is not to follow, the Lord's Prayer is now said.

The Priest concludes

The Almighty Lord, who is a strong tower to all who put their trust in him, to whom all things in heaven, on earth, and under the earth bow and obey: Be now and evermore your defense, and make you know and feel that the only Name under heaven given for health and salvation is the Name of our Lord Jesus Christ. *Amen.*

Part III. Holy Communion

If the Eucharist is to be celebrated, the Priest begins with the [Peace and] Offertory.

Any of the forms on pages 34 and 66 may be used, or else the forms in The Book of Common Prayer.

If Communion is to be administered from the reserved Sacrament, the form for Communion under Special Circumstances is used, beginning with the [Peace and] Lord's Prayer on page 22.

If the sick person cannot receive either the consecrated Bread or the Wine, it is suitable to administer the Sacrament in one kind only.

One of the usual postcommunion prayers is said, or the following

Gracious Father, we give you praise and thanks for this Holy Communion of the Body and Blood of your beloved Son Jesus Christ, the pledge of our redemption; and we pray that it may bring us forgiveness of our sins, strength in our weakness, and everlasting salvation; through Jesus Christ our Lord. *Amen.*

The service concludes with a blessing or with a dismissal

Let us bless the Lord.

Thanks be to God.

If a person desires to receive the Sacrament, but, by reason of extreme sickness or physical disability, is unable to eat and drink the Bread and Wine, the celebrant is to assure that person that all the benefits of Communion are received, even though the Sacrament is not received with the mouth.

Prayers for the Sick   *(See also pages 104–111).*

For a Sick Person

O Father of mercies and God of all comfort, our only help in time of need: We humbly beseech thee to behold, visit, and relieve thy sick servant *N.* for whom our prayers are desired. Look upon *him* with the eyes of thy mercy; comfort *him* with a sense of thy goodness; preserve *him* from the temptations of the enemy; and give *him* patience under *his* affliction. In thy good time, restore *him* to health, and enable *him* to lead the residue of *his* life in thy fear, and to thy glory; and grant that finally *he* may dwell with thee in life everlasting; through Jesus Christ our Lord. *Amen.*

For Recovery from Sickness

O God, the strength of the weak and the comfort of sufferers: Mercifully accept our prayers, and grant to your servant N. the help of your power, that *his* sickness may be turned into health, and our sorrow into joy; through Jesus Christ our Lord. *Amen.*

or this

O God of heavenly powers, by the might of your command you drive away from our bodies all sickness and all infirmity: Be present in your goodness with your servant N., that *his* weakness may be banished and *his* strength restored; and that, *his* health being renewed, *he* may bless your holy Name; through Jesus Christ our Lord. *Amen.*

For a Sick Child

Heavenly Father, watch with us over your child N., and grant that *he* may be restored to that perfect health which it is yours alone to give; through Jesus Christ our Lord. *Amen.*

or *this*

Lord Jesus Christ, Good Shepherd of the sheep, you gather the lambs in your arms and carry them in your bosom: We commend to your loving care this child N. Relieve *his* pain, guard *him* from all danger, restore to *him* your gifts of gladness and strength, and raise *him* up to a life of service to you. Hear us, we pray, for your dear Name's sake. *Amen.*

Before an Operation

Almighty God our heavenly Father, graciously comfort your servant N. in *his* suffering, and bless the means made use of for *his* cure. Fill *his* heart with confidence that, though at times *he* may be afraid, *he* yet may put *his* trust in you; through Jesus Christ our Lord. *Amen.*

or *this*

Strengthen your servant N., O God, to do what *he* has to do and bear what *he* has to bear; that, accepting your healing gifts through the skill of surgeons and nurses, *he* may be restored to usefulness in your world with a thankful heart; through Jesus Christ our Lord. *Amen.*

For Strength and Confidence

Heavenly Father, giver of life and health: Comfort and relieve your sick servant N., and give your power of healing to those who minister to *his* needs, that *he* may be strengthened in *his* weakness and have confidence in your loving care; through Jesus Christ our Lord. *Amen.*

For the Sanctification of Illness

Sanctify, O Lord, the sickness of your servant N., that the sense of *his* weakness may add strength to *his* faith and seriousness to *his* repentance; and grant that *he* may live with you in everlasting life; through Jesus Christ our Lord. *Amen.*

For Health of Body and Soul

May God the Father bless you, God the Son heal you, God the Holy Spirit give you strength. May God the holy and undivided Trinity guard your body, save your soul, and bring you safely to his heavenly country; where he lives and reigns for ever and ever. *Amen.*

For Doctors and Nurses

Sanctify, O Lord, those whom you have called to the study and practice of the arts of healing, and to the prevention of disease and pain. Strengthen them by your life-giving Spirit, that by their ministries the health of the community may be promoted and your creation glorified; through Jesus Christ our Lord. *Amen.*

Thanksgiving for a Beginning of Recovery

O Lord, your compassions never fail and your mercies are new every morning: We give you thanks for giving our brother (sister) *N.*, both relief from pain and hope of health renewed. Continue in *him,* we pray, the good work you have begun; that *he,* daily increasing in bodily strength, and rejoicing in your goodness, may so order *his* life and conduct that *he* may always think and do those things that please you; through Jesus Christ our Lord. *Amen.*

Prayers for use by a Sick Person

For Trust in God

O God, the source of all health: So fill my heart with faith in your love, that with calm expectancy I may make room for your power to possess me, and gracefully accept your healing; through Jesus Christ our Lord. Amen.

In Pain

Lord Jesus Christ, by your patience in suffering you hallowed earthly pain and gave us the example of obedience to your Father's will: Be near me in my time of weakness and pain; sustain me by your grace, that my strength and courage may not fail; heal me according to your will; and help me always to believe that what happens to me here is of little account if you hold me in eternal life, my Lord and my God. Amen.

For Sleep

O heavenly Father, you give your children sleep for the refreshing of soul and body: Grant me this gift, I pray; keep me in that perfect peace which you have promised to those whose minds are fixed on you; and give me such a sense of your presence, that in the hours of silence I may enjoy the blessed assurance of your love; through Jesus Christ our Savior. Amen.

In the Morning

This is another day, O Lord. I know not what it will bring forth, but make me ready, Lord, for whatever it may be. If I am able to stand up, help me to stand bravely. If I am to sit still, help me to sit quietly. If I am to lie low, help me to do it patiently. And if I am to do nothing, let me do it gallantly. Make these words more than words, and give me the Spirit of Jesus. Amen.

Communion under Special Circumstances

This form is intended for use with those who for reasonable cause cannot be present at a public celebration of the Eucharist.

When persons are unable to be present for extended periods, it is desirable that the priest arrange to celebrate the Eucharist with them from time to time on a regular basis, using either the Proper of the Day or one of those appointed for Various Occasions. (See pages 87–92) If it is necessary to shorten the service, the priest may begin the celebration at the Offertory, but it is desirable that a passage from the Gospel first be read.

At other times, or when desired, such persons may be communicated from the reserved Sacrament, using the following form.

It is desirable that fellow parishioners, relatives, and friends be present, when possible, to communicate with them.

The Celebrant, whether priest or deacon, reads a passage of Scripture appropriate to the day or occasion, or else one of the following

God so loved the world that he gave his only Son, that whoever believes in him should not perish, but have eternal life.   *John 3:16*

Jesus said, "I am the bread of life, whoever comes to me shall not hunger, and whoever believes in me shall never thirst."   *John 6:35*

Jesus said, "I am the living bread which came down from heaven; if anyone eats of this bread, he will live forever; and the bread which I shall give for the life of the world is my flesh. For my flesh is food indeed, and my blood is drink indeed. Whoever eats my flesh and drinks my blood abides in me, and I in him."   *John 6:51, 55–56*

Jesus said, "Abide in me, as I in you. As the branch cannot bear fruit by itself, unless it abides in the vine, neither can you, unless you abide in me. I am the vine, you are the branches. By this my Father is glorified, that you bear much fruit, and so prove to be my disciples. As the Father has loved me, so have I loved you; abide in my love."   *John 15:4–5a, 8–9*

After the Reading, the Celebrant may comment on it briefly.

Suitable prayers may be offered, concluding with the following or some other Collect

Almighty Father, whose dear Son, on the night before he suffered, instituted the Sacrament of his Body and Blood: Mercifully grant that we may receive it thankfully in remembrance of Jesus Christ our Lord, who in these holy mysteries gives us a pledge of eternal life; and who lives and reigns for ever and ever. *Amen.*

A Confession of Sin may follow. The following or some other form is used (other forms of the General Confession are on pages 36, 38, and 64)

Most merciful God,
we confess that we have sinned against you
in thought, word, and deed,
by what we have done,
and by what we have left undone.
We have not loved you with our whole heart;
we have not loved our neighbors as ourselves.
We are truly sorry and we humbly repent.
For the sake of your Son Jesus Christ,
have mercy on us and forgive us;

that we may delight in your will,
and walk in your ways,
to the glory of your Name. Amen.

The Priest alone says

Almighty God have mercy on you, forgive you all
your sins through our Lord Jesus Christ, strengthen
you in all goodness, and by the power of the Holy
Spirit keep you in eternal life. *Amen.*

*A deacon using the preceding formula substitutes "us" for
"you" and "our" for "your."*

The Peace may then be exchanged.

Celebrant   The peace of the Lord be always with
            you.
Response   And also with you.

*Those present may greet one another in the name of the
Lord.*

The Lord's Prayer is said, the Celebrant first saying

Let us pray in the words our Savior Christ has taught
us.

Our Father, who art in heaven,
  hallowed be thy Name,
  thy kingdom come,
  thy will be done,
    on earth as it is in heaven.
Give us this day our daily bread.
And forgive us our trespasses,
  as we forgive those
    who trespass against us.
And lead us not into temptation,
  but deliver us from evil.
For thine is the kingdom,
  and the power, and the glory,
  for ever and ever. Amen.

or this

Our Father in heaven,
  hallowed be your Name,
  your kingdom come,
  your will be done,
    on earth as in heaven.
Give us today our daily bread.
Forgive us our sins
  as we forgive those
    who sin against us.
Save us from the time of trial,
  and deliver us from evil.
For the kingdom, the power,
  and the glory are yours,
  now and for ever. Amen.

The Celebrant may say the following Invitation

The Gifts of God for the People of God.

and may add

> Take them in remembrance that Christ
> died for you, and feed on him in your
> hearts by faith, with thanksgiving.

The Sacrament is administered with the following or other words

The Body (Blood) of our Lord Jesus Christ keep you in everlasting life. [*Amen.*]

One of the usual postcommunion prayers is then said, or the following

Gracious Father, we give you praise and thanks for this Holy Communion of the Body and Blood of your beloved Son Jesus Christ, the pledge of our redemption; and we pray that it may bring us forgiveness of our sins, strength in our weakness, and everlasting salvation; through Jesus Christ our Lord. *Amen.*

The service concludes with a blessing or with a dismissal

Let us bless the Lord.
Thanks be to God.

Concerning the Rite

The ministry of reconciliation, which has been committed by Christ to his Church, is exercised through the care each Christian has for others, through the common prayer of Christians assembled for public worship, and through the priesthood of the Church and its ministers declaring absolution.

The Reconciliation of a Penitent is available for all who desire it. It is not restricted to times of sickness. Confessions may be heard anytime and anywhere.

Two equivalent forms of service are provided here to meet the needs of penitents. The absolution in these services may be pronounced only by a bishop or priest. Another Christian may be asked to hear a confession, but it must be made clear to the penitent that absolution will not be pronounced; instead, a declaration of forgiveness is provided.

When a confession is heard in a church building, the confessor may sit inside the altar rails or in a place set aside to give greater privacy, and the penitent kneels nearby. If preferred, the confessor and penitent may sit face to face for a spiritual conference leading to absolution or a declaration of forgiveness.

When the penitent has confessed all serious sins troubling the conscience and has given evidence of due contrition, the priest gives such counsel and encouragement as are needed and pronounces absolution. Before giving absolution, the priest may assign to the penitent a psalm, prayer, or a hymn to be said, or something to be done, as a sign of penitence and act of thanksgiving.

The content of a confession is not normally a matter of subsequent discussion. The secrecy of a confession is morally absolute for the confessor, and must under no circumstances be broken.

The Reconciliation
of a Penitent

Form One

The Penitent begins

Bless me, for I have sinned.

The Priest says

The Lord be in your heart and upon your lips that you may truly and humbly confess your sins: In the Name of the Father, and of the Son, and of the Holy Spirit. *Amen.*

Penitent

I confess to Almighty God, to his Church, and to you, that I have sinned by my own fault in thought, word, and deed, in things done and left undone; especially _____. For these and all other sins which I cannot now remember, I am truly sorry. I pray God to have mercy on me. I firmly intend amendment of life, and I humbly beg forgiveness of God and his Church, and ask you for counsel, direction and absolution.

Here the Priest may offer counsel, direction, and comfort.

The Priest then pronounces this absolution

Our Lord Jesus Christ, who has left power to his Church to absolve all sinners who truly repent and believe in him, of his great mercy forgive you all your offenses; and by his authority committed to me, I absolve you from all your sins: In the Name of the Father, and of the Son, and of the Holy Spirit. *Amen.*

or this

Our Lord Jesus Christ, who offered himself to be sacrificed for us to the Father, and who conferred power on his Church to forgive sins, absolve you through my ministry by the grace of the Holy Spirit, and restore you to the perfect peace of the Church. *Amen.*

The Priest adds

The Lord has put away all your sins.

Penitent   Thanks be to God.

The Priest concludes

Go (*or* abide) in peace, and pray for me, a sinner.

Declaration of Forgiveness
to be used by a Deacon or Lay Person

Our Lord Jesus Christ, who offered himself to be sacrificed for us to the Father, forgives your sins by the grace of the Holy Spirit. *Amen.*

Form Two

The Priest and Penitent begin as follows

Have mercy on me, O God, according to your
  loving-kindness; in your great compassion blot
  out my offenses.
Wash me through and through from my
  wickedness, and cleanse me from my sin.
For I know my transgressions only too well, and
  my sin is ever before me.

Holy God, Holy and Mighty, Holy Immortal One, have mercy upon us.

Penitent   Pray for me, a sinner.

Priest

May God in his love enlighten your heart, that you may remember in truth all your sins and his unfailing mercy. *Amen.*

The Priest may then say one or more of these or other appropriate verses of Scripture, first saying

Hear the Word of God to all who truly turn to him.

Come unto me, all ye that travail and are heavy laden, and I will refresh you.   *Matthew 11:28*

God so loved the world, that he gave his only-begotten Son, to the end that all that believe in him should not perish, but have everlasting life.   *John 3:16*

This is a true saying, and worthy of all men to be received, that Christ Jesus came into the world to save sinners.   *1 Timothy 1:15*

If any man sin, we have an Advocate with the Father, Jesus Christ the righteous; and he is the perfect offering for our sins, and not for ours only, but for the sins of the whole world.   *1 John 2:1–2*

The Priest then continues

Now, in the presence of Christ, and of me, his minister, confess your sins with a humble and obedient heart to Almighty God, our Creator and our Redeemer.

The Penitent says

Holy God, heavenly Father, you formed me from the dust in your image and likeness, and redeemed me from sin and death by the cross of your Son Jesus Christ. Through the water of baptism you clothed me with the shining garment of his righteousness, and established me among your children in your kingdom. But I have squandered the inheritance of your saints, and have wandered far in a land that is waste.

Especially, I confess to you and to the Church...

Here the Penitent confesses particular sins.

Therefore, O Lord, from these and all other sins I cannot now remember, I turn to you in sorrow and repentance. Receive me again into the arms of your mercy, and restore me to the blessed company of your faithful people; through him in whom you have redeemed the world, your Son our Savior Jesus Christ. Amen.

The Priest may then offer words of comfort and counsel.

Priest

Will you turn again to Christ as your Lord?

Penitent I will.

Priest

Do you, then, forgive those who have sinned against you?

Penitent I forgive them.

Priest

May Almighty God in mercy receive your confession of sorrow and of faith, strengthen you in all goodness, and by the power of the Holy Spirit keep you in eternal life. *Amen.*

The Priest then lays a hand upon the penitent's head (or extends a hand over the penitent), saying one of the following

Our Lord Jesus Christ, who offered himself to be sacrificed for us to the Father, and who conferred power on his Church to forgive sins, absolve you through my ministry by the grace of the Holy Spirit, and restore you in the perfect peace of the Church. *Amen.*

or this

Our Lord Jesus Christ, who has left power to his Church to absolve all sinners who truly repent and believe in him, of his great mercy forgive you all your offenses; and by his authority committed to me, I absolve you from all your sins: In the Name of the Father, and of the Son, and of the Holy Spirit. *Amen.*

The Priest concludes

Now there is rejoicing in heaven; for you were lost, and are found; you were dead, and are now alive in Christ Jesus our Lord. Go (*or* abide) in peace. The Lord has put away all your sins.

Penitent   Thanks be to God.

Declaration of Forgiveness
to be used by a Deacon or Lay Person

Our Lord Jesus Christ, who offered himself to be
sacrificed for us to the Father, forgives your sins by
the grace of the Holy Spirit. *Amen.*

A Penitential Order: Traditional

For use at the beginning of the Liturgy, or as a separate
service.

A hymn, psalm, or anthem may be sung.

The Celebrant says

      Blessed be God: Father, Son, and Holy
      Spirit.

People   And blessed be his kingdom, now and for
      ever. Amen.

In place of the above, from Easter Day through the Day of
Pentecost

Celebrant	Alleluia. Christ is risen.
People	The Lord is risen indeed. Alleluia.

In Lent and on other penitential occasions

Celebrant	Bless the Lord who forgiveth all our sins.
People	His mercy endureth for ever.

When used as a separate service, the Exhortation, page 316 of The Book of Common Prayer, may be read, or a homily preached.

The Decalogue, page 317 of The Book of Common Prayer, may be said.

The Celebrant may read one of the following sentences

Hear what our Lord Jesus Christ saith:
Thou shalt love the Lord thy God with all thy heart, and with all thy soul, and with all thy mind. This is the first and great commandment. And the second is like unto it: Thou shalt love thy neighbor as thyself. On these two commandments hang all the Law and the prophets.   *Matthew 22:37–40*

If we say that we have no sin, we deceive ourselves, and the truth is not in us; but if we confess our sins, God is faithful and just to forgive us our sins, and to cleanse us from all unrighteousness.   *1 John 1:8, 9*

Seeing that we have a great high priest, that is passed into the heavens, Jesus the Son of God, let us come boldly unto the throne of grace, that we may obtain mercy, and find grace to help in time of need. *Hebrews 4:14, 16*

The Deacon or Celebrant then says

Let us humbly confess our sins unto Almighty God.

Silence may be kept.

Minister and People

Most merciful God,
we confess that we have sinned against thee
in thought, word, and deed,
by what we have done,
and by what we have left undone.
We have not loved thee with our whole heart;
we have not loved our neighbors as ourselves.
We are truly sorry and we humbly repent.

For the sake of thy Son Jesus Christ,
have mercy on us and forgive us;
that we may delight in thy will,
and walk in thy ways,
to the glory of thy Name. Amen.

or this (Another form of the Confession is on page 38)

Almighty and most merciful Father,
we have erred and strayed from thy ways like lost
    sheep,
we have followed too much the devices and desires
    of our own hearts,
we have offended against thy holy laws,
we have left undone those things which we ought
    to have done,
and we have done those things which we ought not
    to have done.
But thou, O Lord, have mercy upon us,
spare thou those who confess their faults,
restore thou those who are penitent,
according to thy promises declared unto mankind
in Christ Jesus our Lord;
and grant, O most merciful Father, for his sake,

that we may hereafter live a godly, righteous, and
   sober life,
to the glory of thy holy Name. Amen.

The Bishop when present, or the Priest, stands and says

The Almighty and merciful Lord grant you absolution and remission of all your sins, true repentance,
amendment of life, and the grace and consolation of
his Holy Spirit. *Amen.*

*A deacon or lay person using the preceding form substi-
tutes "us" for "you" and "our" for "your."*

*[When this Order is used at the beginning of the Liturgy,
the service continues with the Kyrie eleison, the Trisagion, or the Gloria in excelsis.]*

*When used separately, it concludes with suitable prayers,
and the Grace or a blessing.*

Another Form of the Confession

Minister and People

Almighty God,
Father of our Lord Jesus Christ,
maker of all things, judge of all men:

We acknowledge and bewail our manifold sins and
    wickedness,
which we from time to time most grievously have
    committed,
by thought, word, and deed, against thy divine
    Majesty,
provoking most justly thy wrath and indignation
    against us.
We do earnestly repent,
and are heartily sorry for these our misdoings;
the remembrance of them is grievous unto us,
the burden of them is intolerable.
Have mercy upon us,
have mercy upon us, most merciful Father;
for thy Son our Lord Jesus Christ's sake,
forgive us all that is past;
and grant that we may ever hereafter
serve and please thee in newness of life,
to the honor and glory of thy Name;
through Jesus Christ our Lord. Amen.

The Bishop when present, or the Priest, stands and says

Almighty God, our heavenly Father, who of his
great mercy hath promised forgiveness of sins to all

those who with hearty repentance and true faith turn unto him, have mercy upon you, pardon and deliver you from all your sins, confirm and strengthen you in all goodness, and bring you to everlasting life; through Jesus Christ our Lord. *Amen.*

The Holy Communion: Traditional

Offertory Sentences

Following the Ministry of the Word, a Confession of sin [and the Peace], the Celebrant may begin the Offertory with any of the sentences below or on page 41, or with some other sentence of Scripture.

Offer to God a sacrifice of thanksgiving, and make good thy vows unto the Most High.　　*Psalm 50:14*

Ascribe to the Lord the honor due his Name; bring offerings and come into his courts.　　*Psalm 96:8*

Walk in love, as Christ loved us and gave himself for us, an offering and sacrifice to God.　　*Ephesians 5:2*

I beseech you, brethren, by the mercies of God, to present yourselves as a living sacrifice, holy and acceptable to God, which is your spiritual worship. *Romans 12:1*

If thou bring thy gift to the altar, and there rememberest that thy brother hath aught against thee, leave there thy gift before the altar, and go thy way; first be reconciled to thy brother, and then come and offer thy gift.   *Matthew 5:23, 24*

Through Christ let us continually offer to God the sacrifice of praise, that is, the fruit of lips that acknowledge his Name. But to do good and to distribute, forget not, for with such sacrifices God is well pleased.   *Hebrews 13:15, 16*

Worthy art thou, O Lord our God, to receive glory and honor and power; for thou hast created all things, and by thy will they were created and have their being.   *Revelation 4:11*

Thine, O Lord, is the greatness, and the power, and the glory, and the victory, and the majesty. For all that is in the heaven and in the earth is thine. Thine is the kingdom, O Lord, and thou art exalted as head above all.   *1 Chronicles 29:11*

or this bidding

Let us with gladness present the offerings and oblations of our life and labor to the Lord.

The Great Thanksgiving

Eucharistic Prayers I and II

Celebrant	The Lord be with you.
People	And with your spirit.
Celebrant	Lift up your hearts.
People	We lift them up to the Lord.
Celebrant	Let us give thanks unto our Lord God.
People	It is meet and right to do so.

Then, facing the Holy Table, the Celebrant proceeds

It is very meet, right, and our bounden duty, that we should at all times, and in all places, give thanks unto thee, O Lord, holy Father, almighty, everlasting God.

Here a Proper Preface is sung or said on all Sundays, and on other occasions as appointed.

Following the Proper Preface the Service continues on page 49 (Eucharistic Prayer I) or on page 58 (Eucharistic Prayer II)

Preface of the Lord's Day

To be used on Sundays as appointed, but not on the succeeding weekdays

1. Of God the Father

Creator of the light and source of life, who hast made us in thine image, and called us to new life in Jesus Christ our Lord.

or this

2. Of God the Son

Through Jesus Christ our Lord; who on the first day· of the week overcame death and the grave, and by his glorious resurrection opened to us the way of everlasting life.

or this

3. Of God the Holy Spirit

Who by water and the Holy Spirit hast made us a new people in Jesus Christ our Lord, to show forth thy glory in all the world.

Prefaces for Seasons

To be used on Sundays and weekdays alike, except as otherwise appointed for Holy Days and Various Occasions

Advent

Because thou didst send thy beloved Son to redeem us from sin and death and to make us heirs in him of everlasting life; that when he shall come again in power and great triumph to judge the world, we may without shame or fear rejoice to behold his appearing.

Incarnation

Because thou didst give Jesus Christ, thine only Son, to be born for us; who, by the mighty power of the Holy Ghost, was made very Man of the substance of the Virgin Mary his mother; that we might be delivered from the bondage of sin, and receive power to become thy children.

Epiphany

Because in the mystery of the Word made flesh, thou hast caused a new light to shine in our hearts, to give the knowledge of thy glory in the face of thy Son Jesus Christ our Lord.

Lent

Through Jesus Christ our Lord, who was in every way tempted as we are, yet did not sin; by whose grace we are able to triumph over every evil, and to live no longer unto ourselves, but unto him who died for us and rose again.

or this

Who dost bid thy faithful people cleanse their hearts, and prepare with joy for the Paschal feast; that, fervent in prayer and in works of mercy, and renewed by thy Word and Sacraments, they may come to the fullness of grace which thou hast prepared for those who love thee.

Holy Week

Through Jesus Christ our Lord; who for our sins was lifted high upon the cross, that he might draw the whole world to himself; who by his suffering and death became the author of eternal salvation for all who put their trust in him.

Easter

But chiefly are we bound to praise thee for the glorious resurrection of thy Son Jesus Christ our Lord, for he is the very Paschal Lamb, who was sacrificed for us, and hath taken away the sin of the world; who by his death hath destroyed death, and by his rising to life again hath won for us everlasting life.

Ascension

Through thy dearly beloved Son Jesus Christ our Lord; who after his glorious resurrection manifestly appeared to his disciples; and in their sight ascended into heaven, to prepare a place for us; that where he is, there we might also be, and reign with him in glory.

Pentecost

Through Jesus Christ our Lord; according to whose true promise the Holy Ghost came down [on this day] from heaven, lighting upon the disciples, to teach them and to lead them into all truth; uniting peoples of many tongues in the confession of one faith, and giving to thy Church the power to serve thee as a royal priesthood, and to preach the Gospel to all nations.

Prefaces for Other Occasions

Trinity Sunday

For with thy co-eternal Son and Holy Spirit, thou art one God, one Lord, in Trinity of Persons and in Unity of Substance; and we celebrate the one and equal glory of thee, O Father, and of the Son, and of the Holy Spirit.

All Saints

Who, in the multitude of thy saints, hast compassed us about with so great a cloud of witnesses, that we, rejoicing in their fellowship, may run with patience the race that is set before us; and, together with them, may receive the crown of glory that fadeth not away.

A Saint

For the wonderful grace and virtue declared in all thy saints, who have been the chosen vessels of thy grace, and the lights of the world in their generations.

or this

Who in the obedience of thy saints hast given us an example of righteousness, and in their eternal joy a glorious pledge of the hope of our calling.

or this

Because thou art greatly glorified in the assembly of thy saints. All thy creatures praise thee, and thy faithful servants bless thee, confessing before the rulers of this world the great Name of thine only Son.

Apostles and Ordinations

Through the great shepherd of thy flock, Jesus Christ our Lord; who after his resurrection sent forth his apostles to preach the Gospel and to teach all nations; and promised to be with them always, even unto the end of the ages.

Baptism

Because in Jesus Christ our Lord thou hast received us as thy sons and daughters, made us citizens of thy kingdom, and given us the Holy Spirit to guide us into all truth.

Commemoration of the Dead

Through Jesus Christ our Lord; who rose victorious from the dead, and doth comfort us with the blessed hope of everlasting life; for to thy faithful people, O Lord, life is changed, not ended; and when our mortal body doth lie in death, there is prepared for us a dwelling place eternal in the heavens.

Eucharist Prayer I   *Continued*

Eucharistic Prayer II continues on page 58

Therefore with Angels and Archangels, and with all the company of heaven, we laud and magnify thy glorious Name; evermore praising thee, and saying,

Celebrant and People

Holy, holy, holy, Lord God of Hosts:
Heaven and earth are full of thy glory.
Glory be to thee, O Lord Most High.

Here may be added

Blessed is he that cometh in the name of the Lord.
Hosanna in the highest

Then the Celebrant continues

All glory be to thee, Almighty God, our heavenly
Father, for that thou, of thy tender mercy, didst give
thine only Son Jesus Christ to suffer death upon the
cross for our redemption; who made there, by his
one oblation of himself once offered, a full, perfect,
and sufficient sacrifice, oblation, and satisfaction,
for the sins of the whole world; and did institute,
and in his holy Gospel command us to continue, a
perpetual memory of that his precious death and
sacrifice, until his coming again.

At the following words concerning the bread, the Cele-
brant is to hold it, or lay a hand upon it; and at the words
concerning the cup, to hold or place a hand upon the cup
or any other vessel containing wine to be consecrated.

For in the night in which he was betrayed, he took

bread; and when he had given thanks, he brake it, and gave it to his disciples, saying, "Take, eat, this is my Body, which is given for you. Do this in remembrance of me."

Likewise, after supper, he took the cup; and when he had given thanks, he gave it to them, saying, "Drink ye all of this; for this is my Blood of the New Testament, which is shed for you, and for many, for the remission of sins. Do this, as oft as ye shall drink it, in remembrance of me."

Wherefore, O Lord and heavenly Father, according to the institution of thy dearly beloved Son our Savior Jesus Christ, we, thy humble servants, do celebrate and make here before thy divine Majesty, with these thy holy gifts, which we now offer unto thee, the memorial thy Son hath commanded us to make; having in remembrance his blessed passion and precious death, his mighty resurrection and glorious ascension; rendering unto thee most hearty thanks for the innumerable benefits procured unto us by the same.

And we most humbly beseech thee, O merciful Father, to hear us; and, of thy almighty goodness, vouchsafe to bless and sanctify, with thy Word and Holy Spirit, these thy gifts and creatures of bread and wine; that we, receiving them according to thy Son our Savior Jesus Christ's holy institution, in remembrance of his death and passion, may be partakers of his most blessed Body and Blood.

And we earnestly desire thy fatherly goodness mercifully to accept this our sacrifice of praise and thanksgiving; most humbly beseeching thee to grant that, by the merits and death of thy Son Jesus Christ, and through faith in his blood, we, and all thy whole Church, may obtain remission of our sins, and all other benefits of his passion.

And here we offer and present to thee, O Lord, our selves, our souls and bodies, to be a reasonable, holy, and living sacrifice unto thee; humbly beseeching thee that we and all others who shall be partakers of this Holy Communion, may worthily receive the most precious Body and Blood of thy Son Jesus Christ, be filled with thy grace and heavenly benediction, and made one body with him, that he may dwell in us, and we in him.

And although we are unworthy, through our manifold sins, to offer unto thee any sacrifice, yet we beseech thee to accept this our bounden duty and service, not weighing our merits, but pardoning our offenses, through Jesus Christ our Lord;

By whom, and with whom, in the unity of the Holy Ghost all honor and glory be unto thee, O Father Almighty, world without end. *AMEN.*

And now, as our Savior Christ hath taught us, we are bold to say,

People and Celebrant

Our Father, who art in heaven,
   hallowed be thy Name,
   thy kingdom come,
   thy will be done,
     on earth as it is in heaven.
Give us this day our daily bread.
And forgive us our trespasses,
   as we forgive those who trespass against us.
And lead us not into temptation,
   but deliver us from evil.
For thine is the kingdom, and the power, and the
    glory,
   for ever and ever. Amen.

The Breaking of the Bread

The Celebrant breaks the consecrated Bread.

A period of silence is kept.

Then may be sung or said

[Alleluia.] Christ our Passover is sacrificed for us;
Therefore let us keep the feast. [Alleluia.]

*In Lent, Alleluia is omitted, and may be omitted at other
times except during Easter Season.*

*The following or some other suitable anthem may be
sung or said here*

O Lamb of God, that takest away the sins of the
world, have mercy upon us.
O Lamb of God, that takest away the sins of the
world, have mercy upon us.
O Lamb of God, that takest away the sins of the
world, grant us thy peace.

*The following prayer may be said. The People may join in
saying this prayer*

We do not presume to come to this thy Table, O
merciful Lord, trusting in our own righteousness,

but in thy manifold and great mercies. We are not worthy so much as to gather up the crumbs under thy Table. But thou art the same Lord whose property is always to have mercy. Grant us therefore, gracious Lord, so to eat the flesh of thy dear Son Jesus Christ, and to drink his blood, that we may evermore dwell in him, and he in us. *Amen.*

Facing the people, the Celebrant may say the following Invitation

The Gifts of God for the People of God.

and may add   Take them in remembrance that Christ died for you, and feed on him in your hearts by faith, with thanksgiving.

The Bread and the Cup are given to the communicants with these words

The Body of our Lord Jesus Christ, which was given for thee, preserve thy body and soul unto everlasting life. Take and eat this in remembrance that Christ died for thee, and feed on him in thy heart, with thanksgiving.

The Blood of our Lord Jesus Christ, which was shed
for thee, preserve thy body and soul unto everlasting
life. Drink this in remembrance that Christ's Blood
was shed for thee, and be thankful.

or with these words

The Body (Blood) of our Lord Jesus Christ keep you
in everlasting life. [*Amen.*]

or with these words

The Body of Christ, the Bread of heaven. [*Amen.*]
The Blood of Christ, the cup of salvation. [*Amen.*]

After Communion, the Celebrant says

Let us pray.   *The People may join in saying this prayer*

Almighty and everliving God, we most heartily
thank thee for that thou dost feed us, in these holy
mysteries, with the spiritual food of the most precious Body and Blood of thy Son our Savior Jesus
Christ; and dost assure us thereby of thy favor and
goodness towards us; and that we are very members
incorporate in the mystical body of thy Son, the
blessed company of all faithful people; and are also
heirs, through hope, of thy everlasting kingdom.
And we humbly beseech thee, O heavenly Father, so

to assist us with thy grace, that we may continue in that holy fellowship, and do all such good works as thou hast prepared for us to walk in; through Jesus Christ our Lord, to whom, with thee and the Holy Ghost, be all honor and glory, world without end. *Amen.*

The Bishop when present, or the Priest, gives the blessing

The peace of God, which passeth all understanding, keep your hearts and minds in the knowledge and love of God, and of his Son Jesus Christ our Lord; and the blessing of God Almighty, the Father, the Son, and the Holy Ghost, be amongst you, and remain with you always. *Amen.*

or this

The blessing of God Almighty, the Father, the Son, and the Holy Spirit, be upon you and remain with you for ever. *Amen.*

The Deacon, or the Celebrant, may dismiss the people with these words

Let us go forth in the name of Christ.
People   Thanks be to God.

or the following

| Deacon | Go in peace to love and serve the Lord. |
| People | Thanks be to God. |

or this

| Deacon | Let us go forth into the world, rejoicing in the power of the Spirit. |
| People | Thanks be to God. |

or this

| Deacon | Let us bless the Lord. |
| People | Thanks be to God. |

From the Easter Vigil through the Day of Pentecost "Alleluia, alleluia" may be added to any of the dismissals.

The People respond   Thanks be to God. Alleluia, alleluia.

Eucharistic Prayer II   *Continued*

Therefore with Angels and Archangels, and with all the company of heaven, we laud and magnify thy glorious Name; evermore praising thee, and saying,

Celebrant and People

Holy, holy, holy, Lord God of Hosts:

Heaven and Earth are full of thy glory.
Glory be to thee, O Lord Most High.

Here may be added

Blessed is he that cometh in the name of the Lord.
Hosanna in the highest.

Then the Celebrant continues

All glory be to thee, O Lord our God, for that thou
didst create heaven and earth, and didst make us in
thine own image; and, of thy tender mercy, didst
give thine only Son Jesus Christ to take our nature
upon him, and to suffer death upon the cross for our
redemption. He made there a full and perfect sacrifice for the whole world; and did institute, and in his
holy Gospel command us to continue, a perpetual
memory of that his precious death and sacrifice, until his coming again.

*At the following words concerning the bread, the Cele-
brant is to hold it, or lay a hand upon it; and at the
words concerning the cup, to hold or place a hand upon the cup
and any other vessel containing wine to be consecrated.*

For in the night in which he was betrayed, he took bread; and when he had given thanks to thee, he broke it, and gave it to his disciples, saying, "Take, eat, this is my Body, which is given for you. Do this in remembrance of me."

Likewise, after supper, he took the cup; and when he had given thanks, he gave it to them, saying, "Drink this, all of you; for this is my Blood of the New Covenant, which is shed for you, and for many, for the remission of sins. Do this, as oft as ye shall drink it, in remembrance of me."

Wherefore, O Lord and heavenly Father, we thy people do celebrate and make, with these thy holy gifts which we now offer unto thee, the memorial thy Son hath commanded us to make; having in remembrance his blessed passion and precious death, his mighty resurrection and glorious ascension; and looking for his coming again with power and great glory.

And we most humbly beseech thee, O merciful Father, to hear us, and, with thy Word and Holy Spirit, to bless and sanctify these gifts of bread and wine, that they may be unto us the Body and Blood of thy dearly-beloved Son Jesus Christ.

And we earnestly desire thy fatherly goodness to accept this our sacrifice of praise and thanksgiving, whereby we offer and present unto thee, O Lord, our selves, our souls and bodies. Grant, we beseech thee, that all who partake of this Holy Communion may worthily receive the most precious Body and Blood of thy Son Jesus Christ, and be filled with thy grace and heavenly benediction; and also that we and all thy whole Church may be made one body with him, that he may dwell in us, and we in him; through the same Jesus Christ our Lord;

By whom, and with whom, and in whom, in the unity of the Holy Ghost, all honor and glory be unto thee, O Father Almighty, world without end.

AMEN.

And now, as our Savior Christ has taught us, we are bold to say,

Continue with the Lord's Prayer, page 53.

A Penitential Order: Contemporary

For use at the beginning of the Liturgy, or as a separate service.

A hymn, psalm, or anthem may be sung.

Celebrant	Blessed be God: Father, Son, and Holy Spirit.
People	And blessed be his kingdom, now and for ever. Amen.

In place of the above, from Easter Day through the Day of Pentecost

Celebrant	Alleluia. Christ is risen.
People	The Lord is risen indeed. Alleluia.

In Lent and on other penitential occasions

Celebrant	Bless the Lord who forgives all our sins.
People	His mercy endures for ever.

When used as a separate service, the Exhortation, page 316 of The Book of Common Prayer, may be read, or a homily preached.

The Decalogue, page 350 of The Book of Common Prayer, may be said.

The Celebrant may read one of the following sentences

Jesus said, "The first commandment is this: Hear, O Israel: The Lord our God is the only Lord. Love the Lord your God with all your heart, with all your soul, with all your mind, and with all your strength. The second is this: Love your neighbor as yourself. There is no other commandment greater than these." *Mark, 12:29–31*

If we say that we have no sin, we deceive ourselves, and the truth is not in us. But if we confess our sins, God, who is faithful and just, will forgive our sins and cleanse us from all unrighteousness. *1 John 1:8, 9*

Since we have a great high priest who has passed through the heavens, Jesus, the Son of God, let us with confidence draw near to the throne of grace, that we may receive mercy and find grace to help in time of need. *Hebrews 4:14, 16*

The Deacon or Celebrant then says

Let us confess our sins against God and our neighbor.

Silence may be kept.

Minister and People

Most merciful God,
we confess that we have sinned against you
in thought, word, and deed,
by what we have done,
and by what we have left undone.
We have not loved you with our whole heart;
we have not loved our neighbors as ourselves.
We are truly sorry and we humbly repent.
For the sake of your Son Jesus Christ,
have mercy on us and forgive us;
that we may delight in your will,
and walk in your ways,
to the glory of your Name. Amen.

*or the following confession from Prayers of the People,
Form VI, page 393 of The Book of Common Prayer*

Have mercy upon us, most merciful Father;
in your compassion forgive us our sins,
known and unknown,
things done and left undone;
and so uphold us by your Spirit
that we may live and serve you in newness of life,

to the honor and glory of your Name;
through Jesus Christ our Lord. Amen.

The Bishop when present, or the Priest, stands and says

Almighty God have mercy on you, forgive you all
your sins through our Lord Jesus Christ, strengthen
you in all goodness, and by the power of the Holy
Spirit keep you in eternal life. *Amen.*

*A deacon or lay person using the preceding form substi-
tutes "us" for "you" and "our" for "your."*

*[When this Order is used at the beginning of the Liturgy,
the service continues with the Gloria in excelsis, the Kyrie
eleison, or the Trisagion.]*

*When used separately, it concludes with suitable prayers,
and the Grace or a blessing.*

The Holy Communion: Contemporary

Offertory Sentences

Following the Ministry of the Word, a Confession of sin, [and the Peace], the Celebrant may begin the Offertory with one of the following sentences, or one of the sentences on page 40, or with some other sentence of Scripture.

Offer to God a sacrifice of thanksgiving, and make good your vows to the Most High.   *Psalm 50:14*

Ascribe to the Lord the honor due his Name; bring offerings and come into his courts.   *Psalm 96:8*

Walk in love, as Christ loved us and gave himself for us, an offering and sacrifice to God.   *Ephesians 5:2*

I appeal to you, brethren, by the mercies of God, to present yourselves as a living sacrifice, holy and acceptable to God, which is your spiritual worship.
Romans 12:1

If you are offering your gift at the altar, and there remember that your brother has something against you, leave your gift there before the altar and go; first be reconciled to your brother, and then come and offer your gift. *Matthew 5:23, 24*

Through Christ let us continually offer to God the sacrifice of praise, that is, the fruit of lips that acknowledge his Name. But do not neglect to do good and to share what you have, for such sacrifices are pleasing to God. *Hebrews 13:15, 16*

O Lord our God, you are worthy to receive glory and honor and power; because you have created all things, and by your will they were created and have their being. *Revelation 4:11*

Yours, O Lord, is the greatness, the power, the glory, the victory, and the majesty. For everything in heaven and on earth is yours. Yours, O Lord, is the kingdom, and you are exalted as head over all. *1 Chronicles 29:11*

or this bidding

Let us with gladness present the offerings and oblations of our life and labor to the Lord.

The Great Thanksgiving

Eucharistic Prayers A and B

Celebrant	The Lord be with you.
People	And also with you.
Celebrant	Lift up your hearts.
People	We lift them to the Lord.
Celebrant	Let us give thanks to the Lord our God.
People	It is right to give him thanks and praise.

Then, facing the Holy Table, the Celebrant proceeds

It is right, and a good and joyful thing, always and everywhere to give thanks to you, Father Almighty, Creator of heaven and earth.

Here a Proper Preface is sung or said on all Sundays, and on other occasions as appointed.

Following the Proper Preface, the Service continues on page 75 (Eucharistic Prayer A) or on page 84 (Eucharistic Prayer B).

Preface of the Lord's Day

To be used on Sundays as appointed, but not on the succeeding weekdays

1. Of God the Father

For you are the source of light and life; you made us in your image, and called us to new life in Jesus Christ our Lord.

or this

2. Of God the Son

Through Jesus Christ our Lord, who on the first day of the week overcame death and the grave, and by his glorious resurrection opened to us the way of everlasting life.

or this

3. Of God the Holy Spirit

For by water and the Holy Spirit you have made us a new people in Jesus Christ our Lord, to show forth your glory in all the world.

Prefaces for Seasons

To be used on Sundays and weekdays alike, except as otherwise appointed for Holy Days and Various Occasions

Advent

Because you sent your beloved Son to redeem us from sin and death, and to make us heirs in him of everlasting life; that when he shall come again in power and great triumph to judge the world, we may without shame or fear rejoice to behold his appearing.

Incarnation

Because you gave Jesus Christ, your only Son, to be born for us; who, by the mighty power of the Holy Spirit, was made perfect Man of the flesh of the Virgin Mary his mother; so that we might be delivered from the bondage of sin, and receive power to become your children.

Epiphany

Because in the mystery of the Word made flesh, you have caused a new light to shine in our hearts, to give the knowledge of your glory in the face of your Son Jesus Christ our Lord.

Lent

Through Jesus Christ our Lord, who was tempted in

every way as we are, yet did not sin. By his grace we are able to triumph over every evil, and to live no longer for ourselves alone, but for him who died for us and rose again.

or this

You bid your faithful people cleanse their hearts, and prepare with joy for the Paschal feast, that, fervent in prayer and in works of mercy, and renewed by your Word and Sacraments, they may come to the fullness of grace which you have prepared for those who love you.

Holy Week

Through Jesus Christ our Lord. For our sins he was lifted high upon the cross, that he might draw the whole world to himself; and, by his suffering and death, he became the source of eternal salvation for all who put their trust in him.

Easter

But chiefly are we bound to praise you for the glorious resurrection of your Son Jesus Christ our Lord; for he is the true Paschal Lamb, who was sacrificed for us, and has taken away the sin of the world. By his death he has destroyed death, and by his rising to life again he has won for us everlasting life.

Ascension

Through your dearly beloved Son Jesus Christ our Lord. After his glorious resurrection he openly appeared to his disciples, and in their sight ascended into heaven, to prepare a place for us; that where he is, there we might also be, and reign with him in glory.

Pentecost

Through Jesus Christ our Lord. In fulfillment of his true promise, the Holy Spirit came down [on this day] from heaven, lighting upon the disciples, to teach them and to lead them into all truth; uniting peoples of many tongues in the confession of one faith, and giving to your Church the power to serve you as a royal priesthood, and to preach the Gospel to all nations.

Prefaces for Other Occasions

Trinity Sunday

For with your co-eternal Son and Holy Spirit, you are one God, one Lord, in Trinity of Persons and in Unity of Being: and we celebrate the one and equal glory of you, O Father, and of the Son, and of the Holy Spirit.

All Saints

For in the multitude of your saints, you have surrounded us with a great cloud of witnesses, that we might rejoice in their fellowship, and run with endurance the race that is set before us; and, together with them, receive the crown of glory that never fades away.

A Saint

For the wonderful grace and virtue declared in all your saints, who have been the chosen vessels of your grace, and the lights of the world in their generations.

or this

Because in the obedience of your saints you have given us an example of righteousness, and in their eternal joy a glorious pledge of the hope of our calling.

or this

Because you are greatly glorified in the assembly of your saints. All your creatures praise you, and your faithful servants bless you, confessing before the rulers of this world the great name of your only Son.

Apostles and Ordinations

Through the great shepherd of your flock, Jesus Christ our Lord; who after his resurrection sent forth his apostles to preach the Gospel and to teach all nations; and promised to be with them always, even to the end of the ages.

Baptism

Because in Jesus Christ our Lord you have received us as your sons and daughters, made us citizens of your kingdom, and given us the Holy Spirit to guide us into all truth.

Commemoration of the Dead

Through Jesus Christ our Lord; who rose victorious from the dead, and comforts us with the blessed hope of everlasting life. For to your faithful people, O Lord, life is changed, not ended; and when our mortal body lies in death, there is prepared for us a dwelling place eternal in the heavens.

Eucharistic Prayer A   *Continued*

Eucharistic Prayer B continues on page 84

Therefore we praise you, joining our voices with Angels and Archangels and with all the company of heaven, who for ever sing this hymn to proclaim the glory of your Name:

Celebrant and People

Holy, holy, holy Lord, God of power and might, heaven and earth are full of your glory.
   Hosanna in the highest.
Blessed is he who comes in the name of the Lord.
   Hosanna in the highest.

Then the Celebrant continues

Holy and gracious Father: In your infinite love you made us for yourself; and when we had fallen into sin and become subject to evil and death, you, in your mercy, sent Jesus Christ, your only and eternal Son, to share our human nature, to live and die as one of us, to reconcile us to you, the God and Father of all.

He stretched out his arms upon the cross, and offered himself in obedience to your will, a perfect sacrifice for the whole world.

At the following words concerning the bread, the Celebrant is to hold it, or lay a hand upon it; and at the words concerning the cup, to hold or place a hand upon the cup and any other vessel containing wine to be consecrated.

On the night he was handed over to suffering and death, our Lord Jesus Christ took bread; and when he had given thanks to you, he broke it, and gave it to his disciples, and said, "Take, eat: This is my Body, which is given for you. Do this for the remembrance of me."

After supper he took the cup of wine; and when he

had given thanks, he gave it to them, and said, "Drink this, all of you: This is my Blood of the new Covenant, which is shed for you and for many for the forgiveness of sins. Whenever you drink it, do this for the remembrance of me."

Therefore we proclaim the mystery of faith:

Celebrant and People

Christ had died.
Christ is risen.
Christ will come again.

The Celebrant continues

We celebrate the memorial of our redemption, O Father, in this sacrifice of praise and thanksgiving. Recalling his death, resurrection, and ascension, we offer you these gifts.

Sanctify them by your Holy Spirit to be for your people the Body and Blood of your Son, the holy food and drink of new and unending life in him. Sanctify us also that we may faithfully receive this holy Sacrament, and serve you in unity, constancy, and peace; and at the last day bring us with all your saints into the joy of your eternal kingdom.

All this we ask through your Son Jesus Christ. By him, and with him, and in him, in the unity of the Holy Spirit all honor and glory is yours, Almighty Father, now and for ever. *AMEN.*

And now, as our Savior
Christ has taught us,
we are bold to say,

People and Celebrant

Our Father, who art in heaven,
  hallowed be thy Name,
  thy kingdom come,
  thy will be done,
    on earth as it is in heaven.
Give us this day our daily bread.
And forgive us our trespasses,
  as we forgive those
    who trespass against us.
And lead us not into temptation,
  but deliver us from evil.
For thine is the kingdom,
    and the power, and the glory,
    for ever and ever. Amen.

or this

As our Savior Christ
has taught us,
we now pray,

People and Celebrant

Our Father in heaven,
   hallowed be your Name,
   your kingdom come,
   your will be done,
      on earth as in heaven.
Give us today our daily bread.
Forgive us our sins
   as we forgive those
      who sin against us.
Save us in the time of trial,
   and deliver us from evil.
For the kingdom, the power,
   and the glory are yours,
   now and for ever. Amen.

The Breaking of the Bread

The Celebrant breaks the consecrated Bread.

A period of silence is kept.

Then may be sung or said

[Alleluia.] Christ our Passover is sacrificed for us;
Therefore let us keep the feast. [Alleluia.]

*In Lent, Alleluia is omitted, and may be omitted at other
times except during Easter Season.*

*In place of, or in addition to, the preceding, some other
suitable anthem may be used.*

*Facing the people, the Celebrant says the following
Invitation*

The Gifts of God for the People of God.

and may add   Take them in remembrance that
Christ died for you, and feed in him
in your hearts by faith, with
thanksgiving.

*The Bread and the Cup are given to the communicants
with these words*

The Body (Blood) of our Lord Jesus Christ keep you in everlasting life. [*Amen.*]

or with these words

The Body of Christ, the bread of heaven. [*Amen.*]
The Blood of Christ, the cup of salvation. [*Amen.*]

After Communion, the Celebrant says

Let us pray.

Celebrant and People

Eternal God, heavenly Father,
you have graciously accepted us as living members
of your Son our Savior Jesus Christ,
and you have fed us with spiritual food
in the Sacrament of his Body and Blood.
Send us now into the world in peace,
and grant us strength and courage
to love and serve you
with gladness and singleness of heart;
through Christ our Lord. Amen.

or this

Almighty and everliving God,
we thank you for feeding us with the spiritual food
of the most precious Body and Blood
of your Son our Savior Jesus Christ;
and for assuring us in these holy mysteries
that we are living members of the Body of your Son,
and heirs of your eternal kingdom.
And now, Father, send us out
to do the work you have given us to do,
to love and serve you
as faithful witnesses of Christ our Lord.
To him, to you, and to the Holy Spirit,
be honor and glory, now and for ever. Amen.

The Bishop when present, or the Priest, may bless the people.

The Deacon, or the Celebrant, dismisses them with these words.

>Let us go forth in the name of the Christ.

People   Thanks be to God.

or this

Deacon   Go in peace to love and serve the Lord.

People   Thanks be to God.

or this

Deacon   Let us go forth into the world,
>rejoicing in the power of the Spirit.

People   Thanks be to God.

or this

Deacon   Let us bless the Lord.

People   Thanks be to God.

From the Easter Vigil through the Day of Pentecost "Alleluia, alleluia" may be added to any of the dismissals.

The People respond   Thanks be to God. Alleluia, alleluia.

Eucharistic Prayer B   *Continued*

Therefore we praise you, joining our voices with Angels and Archangels and with all the company of heaven, who for ever sing this hymn to proclaim the glory of your Name:

Celebrant and People

Holy, holy, holy Lord, God of power and might, heaven and earth are full of your glory.
  Hosanna in the highest.
Blessed is he who comes in the name of the Lord.
  Hosanna in the highest.

Then the Celebrant continues

We give thanks to you, O God, for the goodness and love which you have made known to us in creation; in the calling of Israel to be your people; in your Word spoken through the prophets; and above all in the Word made flesh, Jesus, your Son. For in these last days you sent him to be incarnate from the Virgin Mary, to be the Savior and Redeemer of the world. In him, you have delivered us from evil, and made us worthy to stand before you. In him, you have brought us out of error into truth, out of sin into righteousness, out of death into life.

At the following words concerning the bread, the Celebrant is to hold it, or lay a hand upon it; and at the words concerning the cup, to hold or place a hand upon the cup and any other vessel containing wine to be consecrated.

On the night before he died for us, our Lord Jesus Christ took bread; and when he had given thanks to you, he broke it, and gave it to his disciples, and said, "Take, eat: This is my Body, which is given for you. Do this for the remembrance of me." After supper he took the cup of wine; and when he had given thanks, he gave it to them, and said, "Drink this, all of you: This is my Blood of the new Covenant, which is shed for you and for many for the forgiveness of sins. Whenever you drink it, do this for the remembrance of me."

Therefore, according to his command, O Father,

Celebrant and People

We remember his death,
We proclaim his resurrection,
We await his coming in glory;

And we offer our sacrifice of praise and thanksgiving to you, O Lord of all; presenting to you, from your creation this bread and wine.

We pray you, gracious God, to send your Holy Spirit upon these gifts that they may be the Sacrament of the Body of Christ and his Blood of the new Covenant. Unite us to your Son in his sacrifice, that we may be acceptable through him, being sanctified by the Holy Spirit. In the fullness of time, put all things in subjection under your Christ, and bring us to that heavenly country where, with [＿＿＿＿ and] all your saints, we may enter the everlasting heritage of your sons and daughters; through Jesus Christ our Lord, the firstborn of all creation, the head of the Church, and the author of our salvation.

By him, and with him, and in him, in the unity of the Holy Spirit all honor and glory is yours, Almighty Father, now and for ever. *AMEN.*

Continue with the bidding and the Lord's Prayer on page 78

A Proper for the Sick

The Collect

Traditional

Heavenly Father, giver of life and health: Comfort and relieve thy sick servants, and give thy power of healing to those who minister to their needs, that those (*or N.,* *or NN.*) for whom our prayers are offered may be strengthened in *their* weakness and have confidence in thy loving care; through Jesus Christ our Lord, who liveth and reigneth with thee and the Holy Spirit, one God, now and for ever. *Amen.*

Contemporary

Heavenly Father, giver of life and health: Comfort and relieve your sick servants, and give your power of healing to those who minister to their needs, that those (or *N.,* or *NN.*) for whom our prayers are offered may be strengthened in *their* weakness and have confidence in your loving care; through Jesus Christ our Lord, who lives and reigns with you and the Holy Spirit, one God, now and for ever. *Amen.*

Preface of the Season

Old Testament Lesson (2 Kings 20:1-5)

A Reading from the Second Book of the Kings: In those days Hezekiah became sick and was at the point of death. And Isaiah the prophet, the son of Amoz, came to him, and said to him, "Thus says the LORD, 'Set your house in order, for you shall die, you shall not recover.'" Then Hezekiah turned his face to the wall, and prayed to the LORD, saying, "Remember now, O LORD, I beseech thee, how I have walked before thee in faithfulness and with a whole heart, and have done what is good in thy sight." And Hezekiah wept bitterly. And before Isaiah had gone out of the middle court, the word of the LORD came to him: "Turn back, and say to Hezekiah the prince of my people, Thus says the LORD, the God of David your father: I have heard your prayer, I have seen your tears; behold, I will heal you; on the third day you shall go up to the house of the LORD."

Psalm 13

How long, O LORD?
will you forget me for ever? *

how long will you hide your face from me?

How long shall I have perplexity in my mind,
and grief in my heart, day after day? *
   how long shall my enemy triumph over me?

Look upon me and answer me, O Lord my God; *
   give light to my eyes, lest I sleep in death;

Lest my enemy say, "I have prevailed over him," *
   and my foes rejoice that I have fallen.

But I put my trust in your mercy; *
   my heart is joyful because of your saving help.

I will sing to the Lord, for he has dealt with
                        me richly; *
   I will praise the Name of the Lord Most High.

or this

Psalm 86   *(Verses 1–7)*

Bow down your ear, O Lord, and answer me, *
   for I am poor and in misery.

Keep watch over my life, for I am faithful; *
   save your servant who puts his trust in you.

Be merciful to me, O Lord, for you are my God; *

I call upon you all the day long.

Gladden the soul of your servant, *
   for to you, O LORD, I lift up my soul.

For you, O Lord, are good and forgiving, *
   and great is your love toward all who call
                              upon you.

Give ear, O LORD, to my prayer, *
   and attend to the voice of my supplications.

In the time of my trouble I will call upon you, *
   for you will answer me.

New Testament Lesson   *(James 5:13–16)*

Is any one among you suffering? Let him pray. Is any
cheerful? Let him sing praise. Is any among you
sick? Let him call for the elders of the church, and let
them pray over him, anointing him with oil in the
name of the Lord; and the prayer of faith will save
the sick man, and the Lord will raise him up; and if
he has committed sins, he will be forgiven. Therefore confess your sins to one another, and pray for
one another, that you may be healed. The prayer of
a righteous man has great power in its effects.

The Gospel *(Mark 2:1–12)*

Deacon or Priest	The Holy Gospel of our Lord Jesus Christ according to Mark.
Response	Glory to you, Lord Christ.

And when Jesus returned to Capernaum after some days, it was reported that he was home. And many were gathered together, so that there was no longer room for them, not even about the door; and he was preaching the word to them. And they came, bringing to him a paralytic carried by four men. And when they could not get near him because of the crowd, they removed the roof above him; and when they had made an opening, they let down the pallet on which the paralytic lay. And when Jesus saw their faith, he said to the paralytic, "My son, your sins are forgiven." Now some of the scribes were sitting there, questioning in their hearts, "Why does this man speak thus? It is blasphemy! Who can forgive sins but God alone?" And immediately Jesus, perceiving in his spirit that they thus questioned within themselves, said to them, "Why do you question thus in your hearts? Which is easier, to say to the paralytic, 'Your sins are forgiven,' or to say,

'Rise, take up your pallet and walk'? But that you may know that the Son of man has authority on earth to forgive sins"—he said to the paralytic—"I say to you, rise, take up your pallet and go home." And he rose, and immediately took up the pallet and went out before them all; so that they were all amazed and glorified God, saying, "We never saw anything like this!"

The Gospel of the Lord.

Response   Praise to you, Lord Christ.

At the Ministry of the Word

The Epistle   *(2 Corinthians 1:3–5)*

Blessed be the God and Father of our Lord Jesus Christ, the Father of mercies and God of all comfort, who comforts us in all our affliction, so that we may be able to comfort those who are in any affliction, with the comfort with which we ourselves are comforted by God. For as we share abundantly in Christ's sufferings, so through Christ we share abundantly in comfort too.

Psalm 91

He who dwells in the shelter of the Most High, *
    abides under the shadow of the Almighty.

He shall say to the LORD,
"You are my refuge and my stronghold, *
    my God in whom I put my trust."

He shall deliver you from the snare of the hunter *
    and from the deadly pestilence.

He shall cover you with his pinions,
and you shall find refuge under his wings; *
    his faithfulness shall be a shield and buckler.

You shall not be afraid of any terror by night, *
    nor of the arrow that flies by day;

Of the plague that stalks in the darkness, *
    nor of the sickness that lays waste at mid-day.

A thousand shall fall at your side
and ten thousand at your right hand, *
    but it shall not come near you.

Your eyes have only to behold *
    to see the reward of the wicked.

Because you have made the LORD your refuge, *
    and the Most High your habitation,

There shall no evil happen to you, *
    neither shall any plague come near your dwelling.

For he shall give his angels charge over you, *
    to keep you in all your ways.

They shall bear you in their hands, *
    lest you dash your foot against a stone.

You shall tread upon the lion and adder; *
    you shall trample the young lion and the serpent
                    under your feet.

Because he is bound to me in love,

therefore will I deliver him; *

    I will protect him, because he knows my Name.

He shall call upon me, and I will answer him; *

    I am with him in trouble;

    I will rescue him and bring him to honor.

With long life will I satisfy him, *

    and show him my salvation.

The Gospel   *(Luke 17:11–19)*

On the way to Jerusalem Jesus was passing along between Samaria and Galilee. And as he entered a village, he was met by ten lepers, who stood at a distance and lifted up their voices and said, "Jesus, Master, have mercy on us." When he saw them he said to them, "Go and show yourselves to the priests." And as they went they were cleansed. Then one of them, when he saw that he was healed, turned back, praising God with a loud voice, and fell on his face at Jesus' feet, giving him thanks. Now he was a Samaritan. Then said Jesus, "Were not ten cleansed? Where are the nine? Was no one found to return and give praise to God except this foreigner?" And he said to him, "Rise and go your way; your faith has made you well."

The Epistle *(Hebrews 12:1–2)*

Therefore, since we are surrounded by so great a
cloud of witnesses, let us also lay aside every weight,
and sin which clings so closely, and let us run with
perseverance the race that is set before us, looking to
Jesus the pioneer and perfecter of our faith, who for
the joy that was set before him endured the cross,
despising the shame, and is seated at the right hand
of the throne of God.

Psalm 103

Bless the LORD, O my soul, *
   and all that is within me, bless his holy Name.

Bless the LORD, O my soul, *
   and forget not all his benefits.

He forgives all your sins *
   and heals all your infirmities;

He redeems your life from the grave *
   and crowns you with mercy and loving-kindness;

He satisfies you with good things, *
   and your youth is renewed like an eagle's.

The LORD executes righteousness *
  and judgment for all who are oppressed.

He made his ways known to Moses *
  and his works to the children of Israel.

The LORD is full of compassion and mercy, *
  slow to anger and of great kindness.

He will not always accuse us, *
  nor will he keep his anger for ever.

He has not dealt with us according to our sins, *
  nor rewarded us according to our wickedness.

For as the heavens are high above the earth, *
  so is his mercy great upon those who fear him.

As far as the east is from the west, *
  so far has he removed our sins from us.

As a father cares for his children, *
  so does the LORD care for those who fear him.

For he himself knows whereof we are made; *
  he remembers that we are but dust.

Our days are like the grass; *
  we flourish like a flower of the field;

When the wind goes over it, it is gone, *
  and its place shall know it no more.

But the merciful goodness of the Lord endures for
              ever on those who fear him, *
  and his righteousness on children's children;

On those who keep his covenant *
  and remember his commandments and do them.

The LORD has set his throne in heaven, *
  and his kingship has dominion over all.

Bless the LORD, you angels of his,
you mighty ones who do his bidding, *
  and hearken to the voice of his word.

Bless the LORD, all you his hosts, *
  you ministers of his who do his will.

Bless the LORD, all you works of his,
in all places of his dominion; *
  bless the LORD, O my soul.

The Gospel *(Matthew 9:2–8)*

[And getting into a boat Jesus crossed over and came
to his own city.] And behold, they brought to him a
paralytic, lying on his bed; and when Jesus saw their

faith he said to the paralytic, "Take heart, my son; your sins are forgiven." And behold, some of the scribes said to themselves, "This man is blaspheming." But Jesus, knowing their thoughts, said, "Why do you think evil in your hearts? For which is easier, to say, 'Your sins are forgiven,' or to say, 'Rise and walk'? But that you may know that the Son of man has authority on earth to forgive sins"—he then said to the paralytic—"Rise, take up your bed and go home." And he rose and went home. When the crowds saw it, they were afraid, and they glorified God, who had given such authority to men.

The Epistle *(James 5:14–16)*

Is any among you sick? Let him call for the elders of the church, and let them pray over him, anointing him with oil in the name of the Lord; and the prayer of faith will save the sick man, and the Lord will raise him up; and if he has committed sins, he will be forgiven. Therefore confess your sins to one another, and pray for one another, that you may be healed. The prayer of a righteous man has great power in its effects.

Psalm 23   *(or the text on page 101)*

The Lord is my shepherd; *
   I shall not be in want.

He makes me lie down in green pastures *
   and leads me beside still waters.

He revives my soul *
   and guides me along right pathways for his
               Name's sake.

Though I walk through the valley of the shadow
            of death,
I shall fear no evil; *
   for you are with me;
   your rod and your staff, they comfort me.

You spread a table before me in the presence of
            those who trouble me; *
   you have anointed my head with oil,
   and my cup is running over.

Surely your goodness and mercy shall follow me
            all the days of my life, *
   and I will dwell in the house of the LORD for ever.

Psalm 23   *King James Version*

The LORD is my shepherd; *
   I shall not want.

He maketh me to lie down in green pastures; *
   and leads me beside the still waters.

He restoreth my soul; *
   he leadeth me in the paths of righteousness for his
               Name's sake.

Yea, though I walk through the valley of the shadow
               of death,
I will fear no evil *
   for thou art with me;
   thy rod and thy staff, they comfort me.

Thou preparest a table before me in the presence
               of mine enemies; *
   thou anointest my head with oil;
   my cup runneth over.

Surely goodness and mercy shall follow me all the
               days of my life, *
   and I will dwell in the house of the LORD for ever.

The Gospel *(Mark 6:7, 12–13)*

And Jesus called to him the twelve, and began to send them out two by two, and gave them authority over the unclean spirits. [He charged them to take nothing for their journey except a staff; no bread, no bag, no money in their belts; but to wear sandals and not put on two tunics. And he said to them, "Where you enter a house, stay there until you leave the place. And if any place will not receive you and they refuse to hear you, when you leave, shake off the dust that is on your feet for a testimony against them."] So they went out and preached that men should repent. And they cast out many demons, and anointed with oil many that were sick and healed them.

The Epistle *(1 John 5:13–15)*

I write this to you who believe in the name of the Son of God, that you may know that you have eternal life. And this is the confidence which we have in him, that if we ask anything according to his will he hears us. And if we know that he hears us in what-

ever we ask, we know that we have obtained the
requests made of him.

Psalm 145 *(Verses 14–22)*

The LORD is faithful in all his words *
    and merciful in all his deeds.

The LORD upholds all those who fall; *
    he lifts up those who are bowed down.

The eyes of all wait upon you, O LORD, *
    and you give them their food in due season.

You open wide your hand *
    and satisfy the needs of every living creature.

The LORD is righteous in all his ways *
    and loving in all his works.

The LORD is near to those who call upon him, *
    to all who call upon him faithfully.

He fulfills the desires of those who fear him; *
    he hears their cry and helps them.

The LORD preserves all those who love him, *
    but he destroys the wicked.

My mouth shall speak the praise of the LORD; *
    let all flesh bless his holy Name for ever and ever.

The Gospel *(John 6:47–51)*

Jesus said, "Truly, truly, I say to you, he who believes has eternal life. I am the bread of life. Your fathers ate the manna in the wilderness, and they died. This is the bread which comes down from heaven, that a man may eat of it and not die. I am the living bread which came down from heaven; if any one eats of this bread, he will live for ever; and the bread which I shall give for the life of the world is my flesh."

Other Prayers

A Collect of the Passion

Almighty God, whose most dear Son went not up to joy but first he suffered pain, and entered not into glory before he was crucified: Mercifully grant that we, walking in the way of the cross, may find it none other than the way of life and peace; through Jesus Christ your Son our Lord. *Amen.*

An Evening Intercession

Keep watch, dear Lord, with those who work, or watch, or weep this night, and give your angels charge over those who sleep. Tend the sick, Lord Christ; give rest to the weary, bless the dying, soothe the suffering, pity the afflicted, shield the joyous; and all for your love's sake. *Amen.*

For those we Love

Almighty God, we entrust all who are dear to us to *thy* never-failing care and love, for this life and the life to come, knowing that *thou art* doing for them better things than we can desire or pray for; through Jesus Christ our Lord. *Amen.*

For a Person in Trouble or Bereavement

O merciful Father, who hast taught us in thy holy Word that thou dost not willingly afflict or grieve the children of men: Look with pity upon the sorrows of thy servant for whom our prayers are offered. Remember *him,* O Lord, in mercy, nourish *his* soul with patience, comfort *him* with a sense of thy goodness, lift up thy countenance upon *him,* and give *him* peace, through Jesus Christ our Lord. *Amen.*

For Guidance

O God, by whom the meek are guided in judgment, and light *riseth* up in darkness for the godly: Grant us, in all our doubts and uncertainties, the grace to ask what *thou wouldest* have us to do, that the Spirit of wisdom may save us from all false choices, and that in *thy* light we may see light, and in *thy* straight path may not stumble; through Jesus Christ our Lord. *Amen.*

For Guidance

Direct us, O Lord, in all our doings with *thy* most gracious favor, and further us with *thy* continual help; that in all our works begun, continued, and ended in *thee,* we may glorify *thy* holy Name, and finally, by *thy* mercy, obtain everlasting life; through Jesus Christ our Lord. *Amen.*

For Quiet Confidence

O God of peace, *who hast* taught us that in returning and rest we shall be saved, in quietness and in confidence shall be our strength: By the might of *thy* Spirit lift us, we pray *thee,* to *thy* presence, where we may be still and know that *thou art* God; through Jesus Christ our Lord. *Amen.*

For Protection

Assist us mercifully, O Lord, in these our supplications and prayers, and dispose of the way of *thy* servants towards the attainment of everlasting salvation; that, among all changes of this mortal life, they may ever be defended by *thy* gracious and ready help; through Jesus Christ our Lord. *Amen.*

For the Answering of Prayer

Almighty God, to whom our needs are known before we ask, help us to ask only what accords with *your* will; and those good things which we dare not, or in our blindness cannot ask, grant us for the sake of *your* Son Jesus Christ our Lord. *Amen.*

For the Answering of Prayer

O Lord our God, accept the fervent prayers of *your* people; in the multitude of *your* mercies, look with compassion upon us and all who turn to *you* for help; for *you are* gracious, O lover of souls, and to *you* we give glory, Father, Son, and Holy Spirit, now and for ever. *Amen.*

For the Coming of the Kingdom

Hasten, O Father, the coming of *thy* kingdom; and grant that we *thy* servants, who now live by faith, may with joy behold *thy* Son at his coming in glorious majesty; even Jesus Christ, our only Mediator and Advocate. *Amen.*

In the Evening

O Lord, support us all the day long, until the shadows lengthen, and the evening comes, and the busy world is hushed, and the fever of life is over, and our work is done. Then in *thy* mercy, grant us a safe lodging, and a holy rest, and peace at the last. *Amen.*

For the Companionship of Saints

Almighty God, by your Holy Spirit you have made us one with your saints in heaven and on earth: Grant that in our earthly pilgrimage we may always be supported by this fellowship of love and prayer, and know ourselves to be surrounded by their witness to your power and mercy. We ask this for the sake of Jesus Christ, in whom all our intercessions are acceptable through the Spirit, and who lives and reigns for ever and ever. *Amen.*

A Prayer attributed to St. Francis

Lord, make us instruments of your peace. Where there is hatred, let us sow love; where there is injury, pardon; where there is discord, union; where there is doubt, faith; where there is despair, hope; where there is darkness, light; where there is sadness, joy. Grant that we may not so much seek to be consoled as to console; to be understood as to understand; to be loved as to love. For it is in giving that we receive; it is in pardoning that we are pardoned; and it is in dying that we are born to eternal life. *Amen.*

A Thanksgiving for Heroic Service

O Judge of the nations, we remember before you with grateful hearts the men and women of our country who in the day of decision ventured much for the liberties we now enjoy. Grant that we may not rest until all the people of this land share the benefits of true freedom and gladly accept its disciplines. This we ask in the Name of Jesus Christ our Lord. *Amen.*

Thanksgiving for the Gift of a Child

See also the Service of Thanksgiving for a Child

Heavenly Father, you sent your own Son into this world. We thank you for the life of this child, *N.*, entrusted to our care. Help us to remember that we are all your children, and so to love and nurture *him,* that *he* may attain to that full stature intended for *him* in your eternal kingdom; for the sake of your dear Son, Jesus Christ our Lord. *Amen.*

Thanksgiving for the Restoration of Health

Almighty God and heavenly Father, we give *thee* humble thanks because *thou hast* been graciously pleased to deliver from *his* sickness *thy* servant *N.*, in whose behalf we bless and praise *thy* Name, Grant, O gracious Father, that *he,* through *thy* help, may live in this world according to *thy* will, and also be partaker of everlasting glory in the life to come; through Jesus Christ our Lord. *Amen.*

For the Saints and Faithful Departed

We give thanks to you, O Lord our God, for all your servants and witnesses of time past; for Abraham, the father of believers, and Sarah his wife; for Moses, the lawgiver, and Aaron, the priest; for Miriam and Joshua, Deborah and Gideon, and Samuel with Hannah his mother; for Isaiah and all the prophets; for Mary, the mother of our Lord; for Peter and Paul and all the apostles; for Mary and Martha, and Mary Magdalene; for Stephen, the first martyr, and all the martyrs and saints in every age and in every land. In your mercy, O Lord our God, give us, as you gave to them, the hope of salvation and the promise of eternal life; through Jesus Christ our Lord, the first-born of many from the dead. *Amen.*

Thanksgiving for the Birth of a Child

The form which follows is a brief form of A Thanksgiving for the Birth or Adoption of a Child, page 439 of The Book of Common Prayer. The complete form is intended for use at a Sunday service in church, following the Prayers of the People preceding the Offertory at the Eucharist, or before the close of the Office at Morning or Evening Prayer.

The brief form may be used in hospital or at home. The Celebrant may begin with the Act of Thanksgiving or with the Prayer "O God, you have taught us." A passage from Scripture may first be read. Either Luke 2:41–51, or Luke 18:15–17, is appropriate.

During the prayers, some parents may wish to express thanks in their own words.

The Gospel *(Luke 2:41–51)*

Now the parents of Jesus went to Jerusalem every year at the feast of the Passover. And when he was twelve years old, they went up according to custom; and when the feast was ended, as they were returning, the boy Jesus stayed behind in Jerusalem. His parents did not know it, but supposing him to be in the company they went a day's journey, and they sought him among their kinsfolk and acquaintances; and when they did not find him, they returned to Jerusalem, seeking him. After three days they found him in the temple, sitting among the teachers, listening to them and asking them questions; and all who heard him were amazed at his understanding and his answers. And when they saw him they were astonished; and his mother said to him, "Son, why have you treated us so? Behold, your father and I have been looking for you anxiously." And he said to them, "How is it that you sought me? Did you not know that I must be in my Father's house?" And they did not understand the saying which he spoke to them. And he went down with them and came to Nazareth, and was obedient to them; and his mother kept all these things in her heart.

or this   *(Luke 18:15–17)*

Now they were bringing even infants to Jesus that he might touch them; and when the disciples saw it, they rebuked them. But Jesus called them to him, saying, "Let the children come to me, and do not hinder them; for to such belongs the kingdom of God. Truly, I say to you, whoever does not receive the kingdom of God like a child shall not enter it."

Act of Thanksgiving

The Celebrant says

Since it has pleased God to bestow upon N. [and N.] the gift of a child, let us now give thanks to him, and say together:

The Song of Mary   *(or else the form on page 129)*

My soul proclaims the greatness of the Lord,
my spirit rejoices in God my Savior; *
    for he has looked with favor on his lowly servant.

From this day all generations will call me blessed: *
    the Almighty has done great things for me,
    and holy is his Name.
He has mercy on those who fear him *
    in every generation.
He has shown the strength of his arm, *
    he has scattered the proud in their conceit.
He has cast down the mighty from their thrones, *
    and has lifted up the lowly.
He has filled the hungry with good things, *
    and the rich he has sent away empty.
He has come to the help of his servant Israel, *
    for he has remembered his promise of mercy,
The promise he made to our fathers, *
    to Abraham and his children for ever.
Glory to the Father, and to the Son, and to the Holy
    Spirit: *
    as it was in the beginning, is now, and will be
    for ever. Amen.

or else Psalm 23 (page 100 or 101) or Psalm 116, (page 173).

The Celebrant then says this prayer

Let us pray.

O God, you have taught us through your blessed Son that whoever receives a little child in the name of Christ receives Christ himself: We give you thanks for the blessing you have bestowed upon this family in giving them a child. Confirm their joy by a lively sense of your presence with them, and give them calm strength and patient wisdom as they seek to bring this child to love all that is true and noble, just and pure, lovable and gracious, excellent and admirable, following the example of our Lord and Savior, Jesus Christ. *Amen.*

Prayers

The Celebrant may add one or more of the following prayers

For a safe delivery

O gracious God, we give you humble and hearty thanks that you have preserved through the pain and anxiety of childbirth your servant *N.*, who desires now to offer you her praises and thanksgivings. Grant, most merciful Father, that by your help she may live faithfully according to your will in this life, and finally partake of everlasting glory in the life to come; through Jesus Christ our Lord. *Amen.*

For the parents

Almighty God, giver of life and love, bless N., and N. Grant them wisdom and devotion in the ordering of their common life, that each may be to the other a strength in need, a counselor in perplexity, a comfort in sorrow, and a companion in joy. And so knit their wills together in your will and their spirits in your Spirit, that they may live together in love and peace in all the days of their life; through Jesus Christ our Lord. *Amen.*

For a child not yet baptized

O eternal God, you have promised to be a father to a thousand generations of those who love and fear you: Bless this child and preserve *his* life; receive *him* and enable *him* to receive you, that through the Sacrament of Baptism *he* may become the child of God; through Jesus Christ our Lord. *Amen.*

For a child already baptized

Into your hands, O God, we place your child *N*. Support *him* in *his* successes and in *his* failures, in *his* joys and in *his* sorrows. As *he* grows in age, may *he* grow in grace, and in the knowledge of *his* Savior Jesus Christ. *Amen.*

The Celebrant may then bless the family

May God the Father, who by Baptism adopts us as his children, grant you grace. *Amen.*

May God the Son, who sanctified a home at Nazareth, fill you with love. *Amen.*

May God the Holy Spirit, who has made the Church one family, keep you in peace. *Amen*

The Peace may be exchanged.

The Minister of the Congregation is directed to instruct the people, from time to time, about the duty of Christian parents to make prudent provision for the well-being of their families, and of all persons to make wills, while they are in good health, arranging for the disposal of their temporal goods, not neglecting, if they are able, to leave bequests for religious and charitable uses.

Daily Devotions for Individuals and Families

These devotions follow the basic structure of the Daily Office of the Church.

When more than one person is present, the Reading and the Collect should be read by one person, and the other parts said in unison, or in some other convenient manner. (For suggestions about reading the Psalms, see page 582 of The Book of Common Prayer.)

For convenience, appropriate Psalms, Readings, and Collects are provided in each service. When desired, however, the Collect of the Day, or any of the Collects appointed in the Daily Offices, may be used instead. The Psalms and Reading may be replaced by those appointed in

a) the Lectionary for Sundays, Holy Days, the Common of Saints, and Various Occasions, page 888 of The Book of Common Prayer.

b) the Daily Office Lectionary, page 934 of The Book of Common Prayer.

c) some other manual of devotion which provides daily selections for the Church year.

A selection of Canticles may be found on pages *125–131*

In the Morning

From Psalm 51

Open my lips, O Lord, *
    and my mouth shall proclaim your praise.
Create in me a clean heart, O God, *
    and renew a right spirit within me.
Cast me not away from your presence *
    and take not your holy Spirit from me.
Give me the joy of your saving help again *
    and sustain me with your bountiful Spirit.
Glory to the Father, and to the Son, and to the
                Holy Spirit: *
    as it was in the beginning, is now, and will be
                for ever. Amen.

A Reading

Blessed be the God and Father of our Lord Jesus
Christ! By his great mercy we have been born anew
to a living hope through the resurrection of Jesus
Christ from the dead.   *1 Peter 1:3*

A period of silence may follow.

A hymn or canticle may be used, the Apostles' Creed, page 131, may be said.

Prayers may be offered for ourselves and others.

The Lord's Prayer

The Collect

Lord God, almighty and everlasting Father, you have brought us in safety to this new day: Preserve us with your mighty power, that we may not fall into sin, nor be overcome by adversity; and in all we do, direct us to be fulfilling of your purpose; through Jesus Christ our Lord. *Amen.*

At Noon

From Psalm 113

Give praise, you servants of the LORD; *
  praise the Name of the LORD.
Let the Name of the LORD be blessed, *
  from this time forth for evermore.
From the rising of the sun to its going down *
  let the Name of the LORD be praised.
The LORD is high above all nations, *
  and his glory above the heavens.

A Reading

O God, you will keep in perfect peace those whose minds are fixed on you; for in returning and rest we shall be saved; in quietness and trust shall be our strength.   *Isaiah 26:3; 30:15*

Prayers may be offered for ourselves and others.

The Lord's Prayer

The Collect

Blessed Savior, at this hour you hung upon the cross, stretching out your loving arms: Grant that all the peoples of the earth may look to you and be saved; for your mercies' sake. *Amen.*

or this

Lord Jesus Christ, you said to your apostles, "Peace I give to you; my own peace I leave with you." Regard not our sins, but the faith of your Church, and give to us the peace and unity of that heavenly City, where with the Father and the Holy Spirit you live and reign, now and for ever. *Amen.*

In the Early Evening

This devotion may be used before or after the evening meal.

O gracious Light,
pure brightness of the everliving Father in heaven,
O Jesus Christ, holy and blessed!

Now as we come to the setting of the sun,
and our eyes behold the vesper light,
we sing your praises, O God: Father, Son, and
    Holy Spirit.

You are worthy at all times to be praised by
    happy voices,
O Son of God, O Giver of life,
and to be glorified through all the worlds.

A Reading

It is not ourselves that we proclaim; we proclaim Christ Jesus as Lord, and ourselves as your servants, for Jesus' sake. For the same God who said, "Out of darkness let light shine," has caused his light to shine within us, to give the light of revelation—the revelation of the glory of God on the face of Jesus Christ. *2 Corinthians 4:5-6*

Prayers may be offered for ourselves and others.

The Lord's Prayer

The Collect

Lord Jesus, stay with us, for evening is at hand and the day is past; be our companion in the way, kindle our hearts, and awaken hope, that we may know you as you are revealed in Scripture and the breaking of bread. Grant this for the sake of your love. *Amen.*

At the Close of Day

Psalm 134

Behold now, bless the LORD, all you servants
 of the LORD, *
  you that stand by night in the house of the LORD.
Lift up your hands in the holy place and bless
  the LORD; *
  the LORD who made heaven and earth bless you
   out of Zion.

A Reading

Lord, you are in the midst of us and we are called by your Name: Do not forsake us, O Lord our God. *Jeremiah 14:9, 22*

The following may be said, or the version on page 131

Lord, you have set your servant free *
    to go in peace as you have promised;
For these eyes of mine have seen the Savior, *
    whom you have prepared for all the world to see:
A Light to enlighten the nations, *
    and the glory of your people Israel.

Prayers for ourselves and others may follow. It is appropriate that prayers of thanksgiving for the blessings of the day, and penitence for our sins, be included

The Lord's Prayer

The Collect

Visit this place, O Lord, and drive far from it all snares of the enemy; let your holy angels dwell with us to preserve us in peace; and let your blessing be upon us always; through Jesus Christ our Lord. *Amen.*

The almighty and merciful Lord, Father, Son, and Holy Spirit, bless us and keep us. *Amen.*

Canticles

Venite   *Psalm 95:1–7; 96:9, 13*

O come, let us sing unto the Lord; *
    let us heartily rejoice in the strength of
                our salvation.
Let us come before his presence
                with thanksgiving, *
    and show ourselves glad in him with psalms

For the Lord is a great God, *
    and a great King above all gods.
In his hand are all the corners of the earth, *
    and the strength of the hills is his also.
The sea is his and he made it, *
    and his hands prepared the dry land.

O come, let us worship and fall down *
    and kneel before the Lord our Maker.
For he is the Lord our God, *
    and we are the people of his pasture
    and the sheep of his hand.

O worship the Lord in the beauty of holiness; *
    let the whole earth stand in awe of him.

For he cometh, for he cometh to judge the earth, *
    and with righteousness to judge the world
    and the peoples with his truth.

Jubilate   *Psalm 100*

Be joyful in the Lord, all you lands; *
    serve the Lord with gladness
    and come before his presence with a song.

Know this: The Lord himself is God; *
    he himself has made us, and we are his;
    we are his people and the sheep of his pasture.

Enter his gates with thanksgiving;
go into his courts with praise; *
    give thanks to him and call upon his Name.

For the Lord is good;
his mercy is everlasting; *
    and his faithfulness endures from age to age.

In Easter Week, in place of an Invitatory Psalm, the following is sung or said. It may be used daily until the Day of Pentecost.

Christ our Passover   *Pascha nostrum*

1 Corinthians 5:7–8; Romans 6:9–11; 1 Corinthians 15:20–22

Alleluia.

Christ our Passover has been sacrificed for us; *
    therefore let us keep the feast,
Not with the old leaven, the leaven of malice
                    and evil, *
    but with the unleavened bread of sincerity
                    and truth. Alleluia.

Christ being raised from the dead will never
                    die again; *
    death no longer has dominion over him.
The death that he died, he died to sin, once for all; *
    but the life he lives, he lives to God.
So also consider yourselves dead to sin, *
    and alive to God in Jesus Christ our
                    Lord. Alleluia.

Christ has been raised from the dead, *
    the first fruits of those who have fallen asleep.
For since by a man came death, *
    by a man has come also the resurrection
                    of the dead.
For as in Adam all die, *
    so also in Christ shall all be made alive. Alleluia.

The First Song of Isaiah   *Ecce, Deus*

Isaiah 12:2–6

Surely, it is God who saves me; *
   I will trust in him and not be afraid.
For the Lord is my stronghold and my
                     sure defense, *
   and he will be my Savior.
Therefore you shall draw water with rejoicing *
   from the springs of salvation.
And on that day you shall say, *
   Give thanks to the Lord and call upon his Name;
Make his deeds known among the peoples; *
   see that they remember that his Name is exalted.
Sing the praises of the Lord, for he has done
                     great things, *
   and this is known in all the world.
Cry aloud, inhabitants of Zion, ring out your joy, *
   for the great one in the midst of you is the
                     Holy One of Israel.

Glory to God   *Gloria in excelsis*

Glory to God in the highest,
   and peace to his people on earth.

Lord God, heavenly King,
almighty God and Father,
   we worship you, we give you thanks,
   we praise you for your glory.

Lord Jesus Christ, only Son of the Father,
Lord God, Lamb of God,
you take away the sin of the world:
   have mercy on us;
you are seated at the right hand of the Father:
   receive our prayer.
For you alone are the Holy One,
you alone are the Lord,
you alone are the Most High,
   Jesus Christ,
   with the Holy Spirit,
   in the glory of God the Father. Amen

The Song of Mary   *Magnificat*

Luke 1:46–55 (Contemporary form on page 113)

My soul doth magnify the Lord, *
   and my spirit hath rejoiced in God my Savior.
For he hath regarded *
   the lowliness of his handmaiden.

For behold from henceforth *
    all generations shall call me blessed.
For he that is mighty hath magnified me, *
    and holy is his Name.
And his mercy is on them that fear him *
    throughout all generations.
He hath showed strength with his arm; *
    he hath scattered the proud in the imagination
        of their hearts.
He hath put down the mighty from their seat, *
    and hath exalted the humble and meek.
He hath filled the hungry with good things, *
    and the rich he hath sent empty away.
He remembering his mercy hath holpen his
    servant Israel, *
    as he promised to our forefathers,
    Abraham and his seed for ever.

Glory to the Father, and to the Son, and to the
    Holy Spirit: *
    as it was in the beginning, is now, and will be
    for ever. Amen.

The Song of Simeon *Nunc dimittis*

Luke 2:29–32

Lord, now lettest thou thy servant depart in peace, *
   according to thy word;
For mine eyes have seen thy salvation, *
   which thou hast prepared before the face
   of all people,
To be a light to lighten the Gentiles, *
   and to be the glory of thy people Israel.

Glory to the Father, and to the Son and to the
   Holy Spirit: *
   as it was in the beginning, is now, and will be
   for ever. Amen.

The Apostles' Creed

I believe in God, the Father almighty,
   creator of heaven and earth.
I believe in Jesus Christ, his only Son, our Lord.
   He was conceived by the power of the Holy Spirit
      and born of the Virgin Mary.
   He suffered under Pontius Pilate,
      was crucified, died, and was buried.
   He descended to the dead.

On the third day he rose again.
He ascended into heaven,
    and is seated at the right hand of the Father.
He will come again to judge the living
    and the dead.
I believe in the Holy Spirit,
    the holy catholic Church,
    the communion of saints,
    the forgiveness of sins,
    the resurrection of the body,
    and the life everlasting. Amen.

From the Psalms

The following Psalms are quoted in whole or in part in the preceding pages. Page numbers are noted in parentheses:

Psalm 13 (88); Psalm 23 (100); Psalm 51:1–3 (29);
Psalm 51:16, 11–13 (119); Psalm 86:1–7 (89);
Psalm 91 (93); Psalm 95:1–7, 96:9, 13 (125);
Psalm 100 (126); Psalm 103 (96); Psalm 113:1–4 (113);
Psalm 134 (123); Psalm 145:14–22 (103).

The Psalms, or portions of Psalms in the following pages have been selected as specially suitable for those who are in hospital, or alone. They may be recited in a group, or read for private meditation. They may also be used in conjunction with the celebration of Holy Communion, or in the context of the Daily Devotions. When at all possible, the use of the complete Psalter from The Book of Common Prayer is highly recommended.

Psalm 4

Answer me when I call, O God, defender of
               my cause; *
  you set me free when I am hard-pressed;
  have mercy on me and hear my prayer.

"You mortals, how long will you dishonor
               my glory, *
  how long will you worship dumb idols
  and run after false gods?"

Know that the LORD does wonders for
               the faithful; *
  when I call upon the LORD, he will hear me.

Tremble, then, and do not sin; *
  speak to your heart in silence upon your bed.

Offer the appointed sacrifices *
    and put your trust in the LORD.

Many are saying, "Oh, that we might see
                better times!" *
    Lift up the light of your countenance upon us,
                O LORD.

You have put gladness in my heart, *
    more than when grain and wine and oil increase.

I lie down in peace; at once I fall asleep; *
    for only you, LORD, make me dwell in safety.

Psalm 8

O LORD our Governor, *
    how exalted is your Name in all the world!

Out of the mouths of infants and children *
    your majesty is praised above the heavens.

You have set up a stronghold against
                your adversaries, *
    to quell the enemy and the avenger.

When I consider your heavens, the work of
                your fingers, *

the moon and the stars you have set in
their courses,

What is man that you should be mindful of him? *
the son of man that you should seek him out?

You have made him but little lower than
the angels; *
you adorn him with glory and honor;

You give him mastery over the works of
your hands; *
you put all things under his feet:

All sheep and oxen, *
even the wild beasts of the field,

The birds of the air, the fish of the sea, *
and whatsoever walks in the paths of the sea.

O LORD our Governor, *
how exalted is your Name in all the world!

Psalm 9   *(Verses 1–2, 9–10, 18–20)*

I will give thanks to you, O LORD, with my
whole heart; *
I will tell of all your marvelous works.

I will be glad and rejoice in you; *
   I will sing to your Name, O Most High.

The LORD will be a refuge for the oppressed, *
   a refuge in time of trouble.

Those who know your Name will put their trust
                     in you, *
   for you never forsake those who seek you,
                     O LORD.

For the needy shall not always be forgotten, *
   and the hope of the poor shall not perish for ever.

Rise up, O LORD, let not the ungodly have the
                     upper hand; *
   let them be judged before you.

Put fear upon them, O LORD; *
   let the ungodly know they are but mortal.

Psalm 11   *(Verses 1–6, 8)*

In the LORD have I taken refuge; *
   how then can you say to me,
    "Fly away like a bird to the hilltop;

For see how the wicked bend the bow

and fit their arrows to the string, *
   to shoot from ambush at the true of heart.

When the foundations are being destroyed, *
   what can the righteous do?"

The LORD is in his holy temple; *
   the LORD's throne is in heaven.

His eyes behold the inhabited world; *
   his piercing eye weighs our worth.

The LORD weighs the righteous as well as
                     the wicked, *
   but those who delight in violence he abhors.

For the LORD is righteous;
he delights in righteous deeds; *
   and the just shall see his face.

Psalm 15

LORD, who may dwell in your tabernacle? *
   who may abide upon your holy hill?

Whoever leads a blameless life and does what
                     is right, *
   who speaks the truth from his heart.

There is no guile upon his tongue;
he does no evil to his friend; *
    he does not heap contempt upon his neighbor.

In his sight the wicked is rejected, *
    but he honors those who fear the LORD.

He has sworn to do no wrong *
    and does not take back his word.

He does not give his money in hope of gain, *
    nor does he take a bribe against the innocent.

Whoever does these things *
    shall never be overthrown.

Psalm 16 *(Verses 1, 5–11)*

Protect me, O God, for I take refuge in you; *
    I have said to the LORD, "You are my Lord,
    my good above all other."

O LORD, you are my portion and my cup; *
    it is you who uphold my lot.

My boundaries enclose a pleasant land; *
    indeed, I have a goodly heritage.

I will bless the LORD who gives me counsel; *
   my heart teaches me, night after night.

I have set the LORD always before me; *
   because he is at my right hand I shall not fall.

My heart, therefore, is glad, and my
                              spirit rejoices; *
   my body also shall rest in hope.

For you will not abandon me to the grave, *
   nor let your holy one see the Pit.

You will show me the path of life; *
   in your presence there is fullness of joy,
   and in your right hand are pleasures for evermore.

Psalm 19

The heavens declare the glory of God, *
   and the firmament shows his handiwork.

One day tells its tale to another, *
   and one night imparts knowledge to another.

Although they have no words or language, *
   and their voices are not heard,

Their sound has gone out into all lands, *
   and their message to the ends of the world.

In the deep has he set a pavilion for the sun; *
   it comes forth like a bridegroom out of
            his chamber;
   it rejoices like a champion to run its course.

It goes forth from the uttermost edge of the heavens
and runs about to the end of it again; *
   nothing is hidden from its burning heat.

The law of the LORD is perfect
             and revives the soul; *
   the testimony of the LORD is sure
             and gives wisdom to
             the innocent.

The statutes of the LORD are just
             and rejoice the heart; *
   the commandment of the LORD is clear
             and gives light to the eyes.

The fear of the LORD is clean
             and endures for ever; *
   the judgments of the LORD are true
             and righteous altogether.

More to be desired are they than gold,
more than much fine gold, *
sweeter far than honey,
than honey in the comb.

By them also is your servant enlightened, *
and in keeping them there is great reward.

Who can tell how often he offends? *
cleanse me from my secret faults.

Above all, keep your servant from
presumptuous sins;
let them not get dominion over me; *
then shall I be whole and sound,
and innocent of a great offense.

Let the words of my mouth and the meditation of
my heart be acceptable in your
sight, *
O Lord, my strength and my redeemer.

Psalm 24

The earth is the Lord's and all that is in it, *
the world and all who dwell therein.

For it is he who founded it upon the seas *
    and made it firm upon the rivers of the deep.

"Who can ascend the hill of the LORD? *
    and who can stand in his holy place?

"Those who have clean hands and a pure heart, *
    who have not pledged themselves to falsehood,
    nor sworn by what is a fraud.

They shall receive a blessing from the LORD *
    and a just reward from the God of
              their salvation."

Such is the generation of those who seek him, *
    of those who seek your face, O God of Jacob.

Lift up your heads, O gates;
lift them high, O everlasting doors; *
    and the King of glory shall come in.

"Who is this King of glory?" *
   "The LORD, strong and mighty,
   the LORD, mighty in battle."

Lift up your heads, O gates;
lift them high, O everlasting doors; *
    and the King of glory shall come in.

"Who is he, this King of glory?" *
   "The LORD of hosts,
      he is the King of glory."

Psalm 27   *(Verses 1–13, 17, 18)*

The LORD is my light and my salvation;
whom then shall I fear? *
   the LORD is the strength of my life;
   of whom then shall I be afraid?

When evildoers came upon me to eat up my flesh, *
   it was they, my foes and my adversaries, who
                    stumbled and fell.

Though an army should encamp against me, *
   yet my heart shall not be afraid;

And though war should rise up against me, *
   yet will I put my trust in him.

One thing have I asked of the LORD;
one thing I seek;
   that I may dwell in the house of the LORD all the
                    days of my life;

To behold the fair beauty of the LORD *
  and to seek him in his temple.

For in the day of trouble he shall keep me safe
                in his shelter; *
  he shall hide me in the secrecy of his dwelling
  and set me high upon a rock.

Even now he lifts up my head *
  above my enemies round about me.

Therefore I will offer in his dwelling an oblation
with sounds of great gladness; *
  I will sing and make music to the LORD.

Hearken to my voice, O LORD, when I call; *
  have mercy on me and answer me.

You speak in my heart and say, "Seek my face." *
  Your face, LORD, will I seek.

Hide not your face from me, *
  nor turn away your servant in displeasure.

You have been my helper;
cast me not away; *
  do not forsake me, O God of my salvation.

What if I had not believed

that I should see the goodness of the LORD *
   in the land of the living!

O tarry and await the LORD's pleasure;
be strong, and he shall comfort your heart; *
   wait patiently for the LORD.

Psalm 30

I will exalt you, O LORD,
because you have lifted me up *
   and have not let my enemies triumph over me.

O LORD my God, I cried out to you, *
   and you restored me to health.

You brought me up, O LORD, from the dead; *
   you restored my life as I was going down to
                        the grave,

Sing to the LORD you servants of his; *
   give thanks for the remembrance of his holiness.

For his wrath endures but the twinkling of an eye, *
   his favor for a lifetime.

Weeping may spend the night, *
   but joy comes in the morning.

While I felt secure, I said,
"I shall never be disturbed. *
    You, LORD, with your favor, made me as strong as
        the mountains."

Then you hid your face, *
    and I was filled with fear.

I cried to you, O LORD; *
    I pleaded with the Lord, saying,

"What profit is there in my blood, if I go down
        to the Pit? *
    will the dust praise you or declare
        your faithfulness?

Hear O LORD, and have mercy upon me; *
    O LORD, be my helper."

You have turned my wailing into dancing; *
    you have put off my sack-cloth and clothed me
        with joy.

Therefore my heart sings to you without ceasing; *
    O LORD my God, I will give you thanks for ever.

Psalm 31 *(Verses 1–3, 5, 22–24)*

In you, O Lord, have I taken refuge;
let me never be put to shame; *
    deliver me in your righteousness.

Incline your ear to me; *
    make haste to deliver me.

Be my strong rock, a castle to keep me safe,
for you are my crag and my stronghold; *
    for the sake of your Name, lead me and guide me.

Into your hands I commend my spirit, *
    for you have redeemed me,
    O Lord, O God of truth.

Yet I said in my alarm,
"I have been cut off from the sight of your eyes." *
    Nevertheless, you heard the sound of my entreaty
    when I cried out to you.

Love the Lord, all you who worship him; *
    the Lord protects the faithful,
    but repays to the full those who act haughtily.

Be strong and let your heart take courage, *
    all you who wait for the Lord.

Psalm 33 *(Verses 1–11)*

Rejoice in the LORD, you righteous; *
  it is good for the just to sing praises.

Praise to the LORD with the harp; *
  play to him upon the psaltery and lyre.

Sing for him a new song; *
  sound a fanfare with all your skill upon
                    the trumpet.

For the word of the LORD is right, *
  and all his works are sure.

He loves righteousness and justice; *
  the loving-kindness of the LORD fills the
                    whole earth.

By the word of the LORD were the heavens made, *
  by the breath of his mouth all the heavenly hosts.

He gathers up the waters of the ocean as in
                    a water-skin *
  and stores up the depths of the sea.

Let all the earth fear the LORD; *
  let all who dwell in the world stand in awe of him.

For he spoke, and it came to pass; *
    he commanded, and it stood fast.

The Lord brings the will of the nations to naught; *
    he thwarts the designs of the peoples.

But the Lord's will stands fast for ever, *
    and the designs of his heart from age to age.

Psalm 34 *(Verses 1–14)*

I will bless the Lord at all times; *
    his praise shall be ever in my mouth.

I will glory in the Lord; *
    let the humble hear and rejoice.

Proclaim with me the greatness of the Lord; *
    let us exalt his Name together.

I sought the Lord, and he answered me *
    and delivered me out of all my terror.

Look upon him and be radiant, *
    and let not your faces be ashamed.

I called in my affliction and the Lord heard me *
    and saved me from all my troubles.

The angel of the LORD encompasses those who
fear him, *
and he will deliver them.

Taste and see that the LORD is good; *
happy are they who trust in him!

Fear the LORD, you that are his saints, *
for those who fear him lack nothing.

The young lions lack and suffer hunger, *
but those who seek the LORD lack nothing that
is good.

Come, children, and listen to me; *
I will teach you the fear of the LORD.

Who among you loves life *
and desires long life to enjoy prosperity?

Keep your tongue from evil-speaking *
and your lips from lying words.

Turn from evil and do good; *
seek peace and pursue it.

Psalm 36 *(Verses 5–10)*

Your love, O LORD, reaches to the heavens, *
 and your faithfulness to the clouds.

Your righteousness is like the strong mountains,
your justice like the great deep; *
 you save both man and beast, O LORD.

How priceless is your love, O God! *
 your people take refuge under the shadow of
 your wings.

They feast upon the abundance of your house; *
 you give them drink from the river of
 your delights.

For with you is the well of life, *
 and in your light we see light.

Continue your loving-kindness to those who
 know you, *
 and your favor to those who are true of heart.

Psalm 40 *(Verses 1–6)*

I waited patiently upon the LORD; *
   he stooped to me and heard my cry.

He lifted me out of the desolate pit, out of the mire
      and clay; *
   he set my feet upon a high cliff and made my
      footing sure.
He put a new song in my mouth,
a song of praise to our God; *
   many shall see, and stand in awe,
   and put their trust in the LORD.

Happy are those who trust in the LORD! *
   they do not resort to evil spirits or turn to
      false gods.

Great things are they that you have done, O LORD
      my God!
how great your wonders and your plans for us! *
   there is none who can be compared with you.

Oh, that I could make them known and tell them! *
   but they are more than I can count.

Psalm 42 *(Verses 1–7)*

As the deer longs for the water-brooks, *
  so longs my soul for you, O God.

My soul is athirst for God, athirst for the
              living God; *
  when shall I come to appear before the presence
    of God?

My tears have been my food day and night, *
  while all day long they say to me,
  "Where now is your God?"

I pour out my soul when I think on these things: *
  how I went with the multitude and led them into
    the house of God,

With the voice of praise and thanksgiving, *
  among those who keep holy-day.

Why are you so full of heaviness, O my soul? *
  and why are you so disquieted within me?

Put your trust in God; *
  for I will yet give thanks to him,
  who is the help of my countenance, and my God.

Psalm 43

Give judgment for me, O God,
and defend my cause against an ungodly people; *
    deliver me from the deceitful and the wicked.

For you are the God of my strength;
why have you put me from you? *
    and why do I go so heavily while the enemy
                    oppresses me?

Send out your light and your truth, that they may
                    lead me, *
    and bring me to your holy hill
    and to your dwelling;

That I may go to the altar of God,
to the God of my joy and gladness; *
    and on the harp I will give thanks to you, O God
                    my God.

Why are you so full of heaviness, O my soul? *
    and why are you so disquieted within me?

Put your trust in God; *
    for I will yet give thanks to him,
    who is the help of my countenance, and my God.

Psalm 46

God is our refuge and strength, *
   a very present help in trouble.

Therfore we will not fear, though the earth
                  be moved, *
   and though the mountains be toppled into the
                  depths of the sea;

Though its waters rage and foam, *
   and though the mountains tremble at its tumult.

The LORD of hosts is with us; *
   the God of Jacob is our stronghold.

There is a river whose streams make glad the city
                  of God, *
   the holy habitation of the Most High.

God is in the midst of her;
she shall not be overthrown; *
   God shall help her at the break of day.

The nations make much ado, and the kingdoms
                  are shaken; *
   God has spoken, and the earth shall melt away.

The LORD of hosts is with us; *
    the God of Jacob is our stronghold.

Come now and look upon the works of the LORD, *
    what awesome things he has done on earth.

It is he who makes war to cease in all the world; *
    he breaks the bow, and shatters the spear,
    and burns the shields with fire.

"Be still, then, and know that I am God; *
    I will be exalted among the nations;
    I will be exalted in the earth."

The LORD of hosts is with us; *
    the God of Jacob is our stronghold.

Psalm 57   (Verses 1–2, 6–11)

Be merciful to me, O God, be merciful,
for I have taken refuge in you; *
    in the shadow of your wings will I take refuge
    until this time of trouble has gone by.

I will call upon the Most High God, *
    the God who maintains my cause.

Exalt yourself above the heavens, O God, *

and your glory over all the earth.

My heart is firmly fixed, O God, my heart is fixed; *
   I will sing and make melody.

Wake up, my spirit;
awake, lute and harp; *
   I myself will waken the dawn.

I will confess you among the peoples, O LORD; *
   I will sing praise to you among the nations.

For your loving-kindness is greater than
               the heavens, *
   and your faithfulness reaches to the clouds.

Exalt yourself above the heavens, O God, *
   and your glory over all the earth.

Psalm 62 *(Verses 1–2, 8–9)*

For God alone my soul in silence waits; *
   from him comes my salvation.

He alone is my rock and my salvation, *
   my stronghold, so that I shall not be
               greatly shaken.

In God is my safety and my honor; *

God is my strong rock and my refuge.

Put your trust in him always, O people, *
    pour out your hearts before him, for God is
        our refuge.

Psalm 63   (Verses 1–8)

O God, you are my God; eagerly I seek you; *
    my soul thirsts for you; my flesh faints for you.
    as in a barren and dry land where there is
        no water.

Therefore I have gazed upon you in your holy place, *
    that I might behold your power and your glory.

For your loving-kindness is better than life itself; *
    my lips shall give you praise.

So will I bless you as long as I live *
    and lift up my hands in your Name.

My soul is content, as with marrow and fatness, *
    and my mouth praises you with joyful lips,

When I remember you upon my bed, *
    and meditate on you in the night watches.

For you have been my helper, *
  and under the shadow of your wings I will rejoice.

My soul clings to you; *
  your right hands holds me fast.

Psalm 66 *(Verses 1–11, 15–18)*

Be joyful in God, all you lands; *
  sing the glory of his Name;
  sing the glory of his praise.

Say to God, "How awesome are your deeds! *
  because of your great strength your enemies
      cringe before you.

All the earth bows down before you, *
  sings to you, sings out your Name."

Come now and see the works of God, *
  how wonderful he is in his doing toward
      all people.

He turned the sea into dry land,
so that they went through the water on foot, *
  and there we rejoiced in him.

In his might he rules for ever;
his eyes keep watch over the nations; *

let no rebel rise up against him.

Bless our God, you peoples; *
    make the voice of his praise to be heard;

Who holds our souls in life, *
    and will not allow our feet to slip.

For you, O God, have proved us; *
    you have tried us just as silver is tried.

You brought us into the snare; *
    you laid heavy burdens upon our backs.

You let your enemies ride over our heads;
we went through fire and water; *
    but you brought us out into a place
            of refreshment.

I called out to him with my mouth, *
    and his praise was on my tongue.

If I had found evil in my heart, *
    the Lord would not have heard me;

But in truth God has heard me; *
    he has attended to the voice of my prayer.

Blessed be God, who has not rejected my prayer, *
    nor withheld his love from me.

Psalm 67

May God be merciful to us and bless us, *
   show us the light of his countenance and come
                     to us.

Let your ways be known upon earth, *
   your saving health among all nations.

Let the peoples praise you, O God; *
   let all the peoples praise you.

Let the nations be glad and sing for joy, *
   for you judge the peoples with equity
   and guide all the nations upon earth.

Let the peoples praise you, O God; *
   let all the peoples praise you.

The earth has brought forth her increase; *
   may God, our own God, give us his blessing.

May God give us his blessing, *
   and may all the ends of the earth stand in awe
                     of him.

Psalm 84

How dear to me is your dwelling, O LORD of hosts! *
   My soul has a desire and longing for the courts
                        of the LORD;
   my heart and my flesh rejoice in the living God.

The sparrow has found her a house
and the swallow a nest where she may lay
                        her young; *
   by the side of your altars, O LORD of hosts,
   my King and my God.

Happy are they who dwell in your house! *
   they will always be praising you.

Happy are the people whose strength is in you! *
   whose hearts are set on the pilgrim's way.

Those who go through the desolate valley will find it
                        a place of springs, *
   for the early rains have covered it with pools
                        of water.

They will climb from height to height, *
   and the God of gods will reveal himself in Zion.

LORD God of hosts, hear my prayer; *
   hearken, O God of Jacob.

Behold our defender, O God; *
    and look upon the face of your Anointed.

For one day in your courts is better than
                        a thousand in my own room, *
    and to stand at the threshold of the house of
                        my God
    than to dwell in the tents of the wicked.

For the LORD God is both the sun and shield; *
    he will give grace and glory;

No good thing will the LORD withhold *
    from those who walk with integrity.

O LORD of hosts, *
    happy are they who put their trust in you!

Psalm 92 *(Verses 1–4)*

It is a good thing to give thanks to the LORD, *
    and to sing praises to your Name, O Most High;

To tell of your loving-kindness early in the morning *
    and of your faithfulness in the night season;

On the psaltery, and on the lyre, *
    and to the melody of the harp.

For you have made me glad by your acts, O LORD; *
    and I shout for joy because of the works of
                your hands.

Psalm 93

The LORD is King;
he has put on splendid apparel; *
    the LORD has put on his apparel
    and girded himself with strength.

He has made the whole world so sure *
    that it cannot be moved;

Ever since the world began, your throne has
             been established; *
    you are from everlasting.

The waters have lifted up, O LORD,
the waters have lifted up their voice; *
    the waters have lifted up their pounding waves.

Mightier than the sound of many waters,
mightier than the breakers of the sea, *
   mightier is the LORD who dwells on high.

Your testimonies are very sure, *
   and holiness adorns your house, O LORD,
   for ever and for evermore.

Psalm 98

Sing to the LORD a new song, *
   for he has done marvelous things.

With his right hand and his holy arm *
   he has won for himself the victory.

The LORD has made known his victory; *
   his righteousness has he openly shown in the
                     sight of the nations.

He remembers his mercy and faithfulness to the
                     house of Israel, *
   and all the ends of the earth have seen the victory
                     of our God.

Shout with joy to the LORD, all you lands; *
   lift up your voice, and sing.

Sing to the LORD with the harp, *
   with the harp and the voice of song.

With trumpets and sound of the horn *
   shout with joy before the King, the LORD.

Let the sea make a noise and all that is in it, *
   the lands and those who dwell therein.

Let the rivers clap their hands, *
   and let the hills sing out with joy before the LORD,
   when he comes to judge the earth.

In righteousness shall he judge the world *
   and the people with equity.

Psalm 102   (Verses 1–3, 7, 24–28)

LORD, hear my prayer, and let my cry come
                before you; *
   hide not your face from me in the day of
                my trouble.

Incline your ear to me; *
   when I call, make haste to answer me,

For the days drift away like smoke, *
   and my bones are hot as burning coals.

I lie awake and groan; *
    I am like a sparrow, lonely on a house-top.

And I said, "O my God,
do not take me away in the midst of my days; *
    your years endure throughout all generations.

In the beginning, O LORD, you laid the foundations
of the earth, *
    and the heavens are the work of your hands;

They shall perish, but you will endure;
that all shall wear out like a garment; *
    as clothing you will change them,
    and they shall be changed;

But you are always the same, *
    and your years will never end.

The children of your servants shall continue, *
    and their offspring shall stand fast in your sight."

Psalm 104

Bless the LORD, O my soul; *
    O LORD my God, how excellent is your greatness!
    you are clothed with majesty and splendor.

You wrap yourself with light as with a cloak *
    and spread out the heavens like a curtain.

You lay the beams of your chambers in the
                        waters above; *
    you make the clouds your chariot;
    you ride on the wings of the wind.

You make the winds your messengers *
    and flames of fire your servants.

You have set the earth upon its foundations, *
    so that it never shall move at any time.

You covered it with the Deep as with a mantle; *
    the waters stood higher than the mountains.

At your rebuke they fled; *
    at the voice of your thunder they hastened away.

They went up into the hills and down to the
                    valleys beneath, *
    to the places you have appointed for them.

You set the limits that they should not pass; *
    they shall not again cover the earth.

You send the springs into the valleys; *
    they flow between the mountains.

All the beasts of the field drink their fill from them, *
 and the wild asses quench their thirst.

Beside them the birds of the air make their nests *
 and sing among the branches.

You water the mountains from your dwelling
     on high; *
 the earth is fully satisfied by the fruit of
     your works.

You make grass grow for flocks and herds *
 and plants to serve mankind;

That they may bring forth food from the earth, *
 and wine to gladden our hearts,

Oil to make a cheerful countenance, *
 and bread to strengthen the heart.

The trees of the LORD are full of sap, *
 the cedars of Lebanon which he planted,

In which the birds build their nests, *
 and in whose tops the stork makes his dwelling.

The high hills are a refuge for the mountain goats, *
 and the stony cliffs for the rock badgers.

You appointed the moon to mark the seasons, *
    and the sun knows the time of its setting.

You make the darkness that it may be night, *
    in which all the beasts of the forest prowl.

The lions roar after their prey *
    and seek their food from God.

The sun rises, and they slip away *
    and lay themselves down in their dens.

Man goes forth to his work *
    and to his labor until the evening.

O LORD, how manifold are your works!
in wisdom you have made them all;
    the earth is full of your creatures.

Yonder is the great and wide sea
with its living things too many to number, *
    creatures both small and great.

There move the ships,
and there is that Leviathan, *
    which you have made for the sport of it.

All of them look to you *
    to give them their food in due season.

You give it to them; they gather it; *
    you open your hand, and they are filled with
                good things.

You hide your face, and they are terrified; *
    you take away their breath,
    and they die and return to their dust.

You send forth your Spirit, and they are created; *
    and so you renew the face of the earth.

May the glory of the LORD endure for ever; *
    may the LORD rejoice in all his works.

He looks at the earth and it trembles; *
    he touches the mountains and they smoke.

I will sing to the LORD as long as I live; *
    I will praise my God while I have my being.

May these words of mine please him; *
    I will rejoice in the LORD.

Let sinners be consumed out of the earth, *
    and the wicked be no more.

Bless the LORD, O my soul. *
    Hallelujah!

Psalm 111 *(Verses 1–4, 7–8, 10)*

Hallelujah!
I will give thanks to the LORD with my whole heart, *
   in the assembly of the upright, in
               the congregation.

Great are the deeds of the LORD! *
   they are studied by all who delight in them.

His work is full of majesty and splendor, *
   and his righteousness endures for ever.

He makes his marvelous works to be remembered; *
   the LORD is gracious and full of compassion.

The works of his hands are faithfulness and justice; *
   all his commandments are sure.

They stand fast for ever and ever, *
   because they are done in truth and equity.

The fear of the LORD is the beginning of wisdom; *
   those who act accordingly have a
               good understanding;
   his praise endures for ever.

Psalm 116   *(Verses 1, 4, 10–11, 16–17)*

I love the LORD, because he has heard the voice of
my supplication, *
    because he has inclined his ear to me whenever
I called upon him.

Gracious is the LORD and righteous; *
    our God is full of compassion.

How shall I repay the LORD *
    for all the good things he has done for me?

I will lift up the cup of salvation *
    and call upon the Name of the LORD.

I will fulfill my vows to the LORD *
    in the presence of all his people,

In the courts of the LORD's house, *
    in the midst of you, O Jerusalem.
    Hallelujah!

Psalm 119   *(Verses 105–109, 111–112)*

Your word is a lantern to my feet *
    and a light upon my path.

I have sworn and am determined *
  to keep your righteous judgments.

I am deeply troubled; *
  preserve my life, O LORD, according to your word.

Accept, O LORD, the willing tribute of my lips, *
  and teach me your judgments.

My life is always in my hand, *
  yet I do not forget your law.

Your decrees are my inheritance for ever; *
  truly, they are the joy of my heart.

I have applied my heart to fulfill your statutes *
  for ever and to the end.

Psalm 121

I lift up my eyes to the hills; *
  from where is my help to come?

My help comes from the LORD, *
  the maker of heaven and earth.

He will not let your foot be moved *
  and he who watches over you will not fall asleep.

Behold, he who keeps watch over Israel *
    shall neither slumber nor sleep;

The LORD himself watches over you; *
    the LORD is your shade at your right hand,

So that the sun shall not strike you by day, *
    nor the moon by night.

The LORD shall preserve you from all evil; *
    it is he who shall keep you safe.

The LORD shall watch over your going out and
                    your coming in, *
    from this time forth for evermore.

Psalm 130

Out of the depths have I called to you, O LORD;
LORD, hear my voice; *
    let your ears consider well the voice of
                    my supplication.

If you, LORD, were to note what is done amiss, *
    O Lord, who could stand?

For there is forgiveness with you; *
    therefore you shall be feared.

I wait for the LORD; my soul waits for him; *
   in his word is my hope.

My soul waits for the LORD,
more than watchmen for the morning, *
   more than watchmen for the morning.

O Israel, wait for the LORD, *
   for with the LORD there is mercy;

With him there is plenteous redemption, *
   and he shall redeem Israel from all their sins.

Psalm 139 (Verses 1–17, 22–23)

LORD, you have searched me out and known me; *
   you know my sitting down and my rising up;
   you discern my thoughts from afar.

You trace my journeys and my resting-places *
   and are acquainted with all my ways.

Indeed, there is not a word on my lips, *
   but you, O LORD, know it altogether.

You press upon me behind and before *
   and lay your hand upon me.

Such knowledge is too wonderful for me; *

it is so high that I cannot attain it.

Where can I go then from your Spirit? *
    where can I flee from your presence?

If I climb up to heaven, you are there; *
    if I make the grave my bed, you are there also.

If I take the wings of the morning *
    and dwell in the uttermost parts of the sea,

Even there your hand will lead me *
    and your right hand hold me fast.

If I say, "Surely the darkness will cover me, *
    and the light around me turn to night,"

Darkness is not dark to you;
the night is as bright as the day; *
    darkness and light to you are both alike.

For you yourself created my inmost parts; *
    you knit me together in my mother's womb.

I will thank you because I am marvelously made; *
    your works are wonderful, and I know it well.

My body was not hidden from you, *
    while I was being made in secret
    and woven in the depths of the earth.

Your eyes beheld my limbs, yet unfinished in
the womb;
all of them were written in your book; *
they were fashioned day by day,
when as yet there was none of them.

How deep I find your thoughts, O God! *
how great is the sum of them!

If I were to count them, they would be more
in number than the sand; *
to count them all, my life span would need to be
like yours.

Search me out, O God, and know my heart; *
try me and know my restless thoughts.

Look well whether there be any wickedness in me *
and lead me in the way that is everlasting.

Psalm 146

Hallelujah!
Praise the LORD, O my soul! *
I will praise the LORD as long as I live;
I will sing praises to my God while I have
my being.

Put not your trust in rulers, nor in any child
of earth, *
    for there is no help in them.

When they breathe their last they return to earth, *
    and in that day their thoughts perish.

Happy are they who have the God of Jacob for
their help! *
    whose hope is the LORD their God;

Who made heaven and earth, the seas, and all that is
in them; *
    who keeps his promise for ever;

Who gives justice to those who are oppressed, *
    and food to those who hunger.

The LORD sets the prisoners free;
the LORD opens the eyes of the blind; *
    the LORD lifts up those who are bowed down;

The LORD loves the righteous;
the LORD cares for the stranger; *
    he sustains the orphan and widow,
    but frustrates the way of the wicked.

The LORD shall reign for ever, *
    your God, O Zion, throughout all generations.
    Hallelujah!

Conditional Baptism

If there is reasonable doubt that a person has been baptized with water, "In the Name of the Father, and of the Son, and of the Holy Spirit" (which are the essential parts of Baptism), the person is baptized in the usual manner, but this form of words is used

If you are not already baptized, N., I baptize you in the Name of the Father, and of the Son and of the Holy Spirit.

Emergency Baptism

In case of emergency, any baptized person may administer Baptism according to the following form.

Using the given name of the one to be baptized (if known), pour water on him or her, saying

I baptize you in the Name of the Father, and of the Son, and of the Holy Spirit.

The Lord's Prayer is then said (page 78)

Other prayers, such as the following, may be added

Heavenly Father, we thank you that by water and the Holy Spirit you have bestowed upon this your servant the forgiveness of sin and have raised *him* to the new life of grace. Strengthen *him,* O Lord, with your presence, enfold *him* in the arms of your mercy, and keep *him* safe for ever.

The person who administers emergency Baptism should inform the priest of the appropriate parish, so that the fact can be properly registered.

If the baptized person recovers, the Baptism should be recognized at a public celebration of the Sacrament with a bishop or priest presiding, and the person baptized under emergency conditions, together with the sponsors or godparents, taking part in everything except the administration of the water.

Ministration at the Time of Death

When a person is near death, the Minister of the Congregation should be notified, in order that the ministration of the Church may be provided.

A Prayer for a Person near Death

Almighty God, look on this servant, lying in great weakness, and comfort *him* with the promise of life everlasting, given in the resurrection of your Son Jesus Christ our Lord. *Amen.*

Litany at the Time of Death

When possible, it is desirable that members of the family and friends come together to join the Litany.

God the Father,
Have mercy on your servant.

God the Son.
Have mercy on your servant.

God the Holy Spirit,
Have mercy on your servant.

Holy Trinity, one God,
Have mercy on your servant.

From all evil, from all sin, from all tribulation,
Good Lord, deliver him.

By your holy Incarnation, by your Cross and Passion, by your precious Death and Burial,
Good Lord, deliver him.

By your glorious Resurrection and Ascension, and by the Coming of the Holy Spirit,
Good Lord, deliver him.

We sinners beseech you to hear us, Lord Christ: That it may please you to deliver the soul of your

servant from the power of evil, and from eternal death,
We beseech you to hear us, good Lord.

That it may please you mercifully to pardon all *his* sins,
We beseech you to hear us, good Lord.

That it may please you to grant *him* a place of refreshment and everlasting blessedness,
We beseech you to hear us, good Lord.

That it may please you to give *him* joy and gladness in your kingdom, with your saints in light,
We beseech you to hear us, good Lord.

Jesus, Lamb of God:
Have mercy on him.

Jesus, bearer of our sins:
Have mercy on him.

Jesus, redeemer of the world:
Give him *your peace.*

Lord, have mercy.
Christ, have mercy.
Lord, have mercy.

Our Father, who art in heaven,
    hallowed be thy Name,
    thy kingdom come,
    thy will be done,
        on earth as it is in heaven.
Give us this day our daily bread.
And forgive us our trespasses,
    as we forgive those
        who trespass against us.
And lead us not into temptation,
    but deliver us from evil.

or this

Our Father in heaven,
    hallowed be your Name,
    your kingdom come,
    your will be done,
        on earth as in heaven.
Give us today our daily bread.
Forgive us our sins
    as we forgive those
        who sin against us.
Save us in the time of trial,
    and deliver us from evil.

184 *At Time of Death*

The Officiant says this Collect

Let us pray.

Deliver your servant, *N.*, O Sovereign Lord Christ,
from all evil, and set *him* free from every bond; that
he may rest with all your saints in the eternal habita-
tions; where with the Father and the Holy Spirit you
live and reign, one God, for ever and ever. *Amen.*

A Commendation at the Time of Death

Depart, O Christian soul, out of this world;
In the name of God the Father Almighty who
   created you;
In the name of Jesus Christ who redeemed you;
In the name of the Holy Spirit who sanctifies you.
May your rest be this day in peace,
   and your dwelling place in the Paradise of God.

A Commendatory Prayer

Into your hands, O merciful Savior, we commend
your servant *N.* Acknowledge, we humbly beseech
you, a sheep of your own fold, a lamb of your own
flock, a sinner of your own redeeming. Receive *him*

into the arms of your mercy, into the blessed rest of everlasting peace, and into the glorious company of the saints in light. *Amen.*

May *his* soul and the souls of all departed, through the mercy of God, rest in peace. *Amen.*